THE BOOK OF PERCUSSION PEDAGOGY

A Step-By-Step Approach for Teachers & Performers

The Common Elements Approach

Cort McClaren

ISBN #0-9723391-0-8

CAP 02900

Cover Design: Ed Morgan of navyblue design
Photography: Heather Rabalais
Page Layout and Typesetting: Nathan Daughtrey
Model for Photography: Michael Ptacin

DEDICATED TO

Gene Clapp, Paul Fry, Richard Gipson, Joseph Graves, Dan King, Robert Lee, Pat Tallarico

Richard Gipson's philosophy of percussion pedagogy had a tremendous impact on the content of this document. I am grateful for the guidance, exemplary role model, and superb musicianship of Joseph Graves, my high school band director, supervisor of student teaching and friend. Robert Lee was my first percussion teacher whom I have continued to admire and hold with utmost respect. He is an ideal role model for any aspiring musician. Gene Clapp was my mentor. I learned professional courage, dedication to individual excellence, and a tremendous sense of pride in being a teacher from Gene. Paul Fry never gave up on a student or a better idea. He always demonstrated kindness and tolerance while instilling excellence. Dan King was my first professional colleague. He taught me tolerance and the joy of helping others reach their fullest potential. From Pat Tallarico I learned to "go beyond," to constantly examine the status quo in an effort to provide a better learning environment for our students.

I owe the inspiration for a career in music to the gentlemen listed above.

- Cort McClaren

SPECIAL THANKS

Diane Cash, Andrew Dancy, Nathan Daughtrey, Danny Frye, Tammy Fisher, Laura Franklin, Jonan Keeny, Michael Lasley, Amanda Swift, and Gary Westbrook had a tremendous influence on the content and design of this document. They are dedicated professionals, each pursuing his/her personal journey toward excellence.

PURPOSE

The purpose of this book is to provide basic information about teaching percussion. The intent is to go beyond providing pictures and illustrations of instruments. The intent is

- to stimulate one to think about the role of percussion in school settings,
- to encourage teachers to provide activities in their individual learning environments that enable young percussionists to realize their fullest potential, and
- to recognize the similarities and differences among the various categories of percussion performance so that the study of percussion might be reduced to a few COMMON ELEMENTS that will transfer to all percussion performance.

This document does not contain all knowledge about percussion pedagogy, percussion performance, or percussion instruments. Rather, it contains essential information that anyone teaching percussion in a school or private situation needs to know and use.

TABLE OF CONTENTS

CHAPTER 1
COMMON ELEMENTS IN PERCUSSION PERFORMANCE

CHAPTER 2
HOW TO DEVELOP A PERCUSSION SECTION

CHAPTER 3
SNARE DRUM

CHAPTER 4
TIMPANI

CHAPTER 5
KEYBOARD PERCUSSION

CHAPTER 6
BASIC ACCESSORY INSTRUMENTS

CHAPTER 7
DRUM SET

CHAPTER 8
HOW TO APPLY THE COMMON ELEMENTS APPROACH IN A REHEARSAL SITUATION

APPENDICES

HOW TO USE THIS BOOK

The ***Book of Percussion Pedagogy*** is intended as a text for an undergraduate Percussion Methods Class, as well as a resource for experienced educators and percussionists to supplement their established teaching style. Each chapter is presented in a logical sequence based on The Common Elements approach.

As a Text for An Undergraduate Percussion Methods Class

Instructors may choose from several models in terms of the order in which the information is presented to a Percussion Methods Class. The instructor's model is determined by available instruments, facilities, and number of class meetings during the course of study.

Model A Some instructors may choose to start at the beginning of the book and progress through each chapter in order.

Model B Some instructors may choose to present the information chapter-by-chapter according to their own predetermined order. In this case, the instructor is advised to throughly instill a working knowledge of the Common Elements before undertaking other activities.

Model C Some instructors may select the approach given below.

1. Introduce the six Common Elements. Ask the students to memorize the Common Elements and their sub-areas.

2. Cover the element of Posture on snare drum, timpani, keyboard percussion, and drum set. Then cover the element of Grip on snare drum, timpani, keyboard, drum set, and so on, until the Common Elements have been covered for all instruments.

3. Introduce applications of the Common Elements in typical rehearsal settings.

4. Introduce applications of the Common Elements to accessory instruments.

Model D Approach the percussion methods class as a beginning percussion section in a school setting. (This method will be most effective with smaller classes of ten or under.) Assign a specified number of students to snare drum, timpani, keyboard percussion, and accessories. For example, in a class of ten students, assign one to timpani, three to snare drum, three to keyboard percussion, and three to accessory instruments. Cover the COMMON ELEMENTS for each instrument as you would in a normal band rehearsal in a school setting. When the students are able to apply knowledge from one Common Element, rotate to different instruments until each Common Element has been thoroughly covered by each student for each primary instrument. When using this scenario, the instuctor is advised to play easy percussion ensemble literature during each rotation in an effort to "apply" the knowledge to practical settings. In this scenario, each of the Common Elements will be covered for each instrument simultaneously, and the class will rotate among instruments as they would in a school setting.

Chapter 1

COMMON ELEMENTS IN PERCUSSION PERFORMANCE

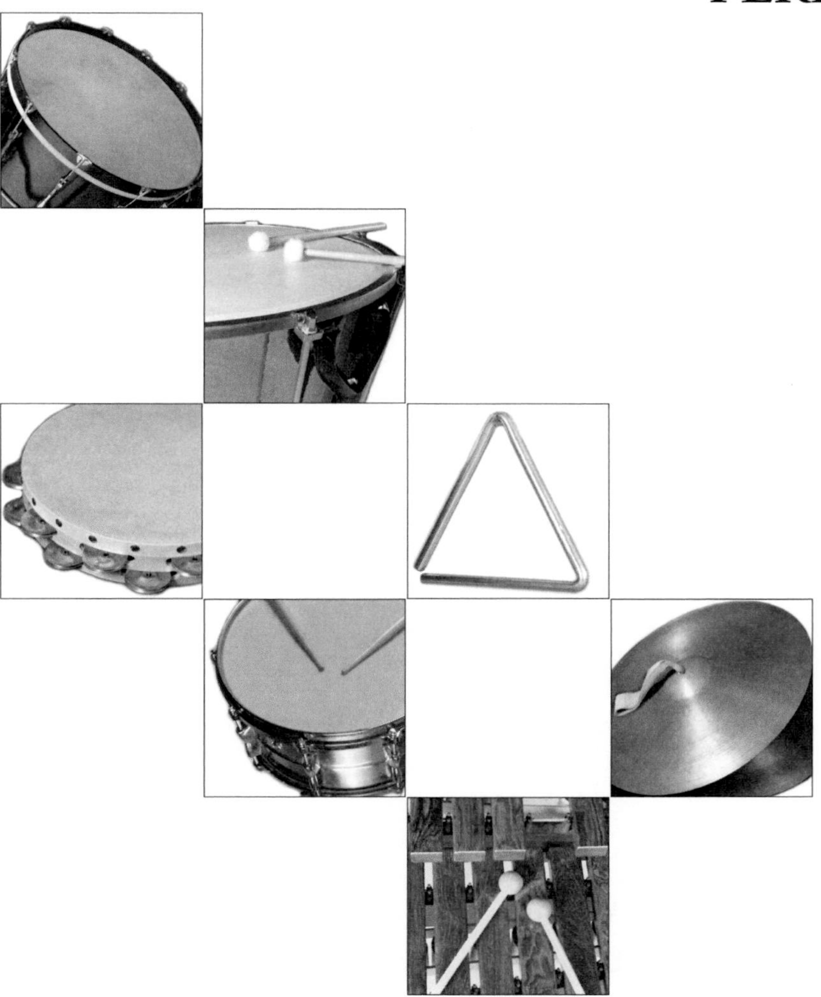

Chapter 1

COMMON ELEMENTS IN PERCUSSION PERFORMANCE

There are many instruments in the percussion family, resulting in a tremendous amount of knowledge to learn - at first glance. However, information about percussion performance can be reduced to a few elements common to all percussion instruments. An approach to percussion pedagogy that focuses on these COMMON ELEMENTS will have tremendous benefit for educators and students. Using the common elements as the basis for teaching percussion will allow teachers to work with all percussion instruments using the same method. Several percussion instruments can be taught and learned simultaneously as long as the information is introduced in an intellectually honest way using the Common Elements approach.

Memorize the following information:

POSTURE	The physical relationship between a performer and the instrument. Posture includes the height of an instrument, the distance between the performer and an instrument, the playing area of a given instrument, as well as the general position of the body or one of its parts. The instrument should always be adjusted to the performer.
GRIP	Method of holding a stick (mallet). Matched Grip is recommended for all percussion performance.
STRIKING MOTION	Striking motion refers to the method of "hitting" an instrument. Piston Motion is recommended for all percussion performance.
VOLUME/DYNAMICS	Volume is determined by the height of the stick and the velocity with which the stick moves toward the surface being struck.
STICKING	Sticking refers to the sequence of right and left hand movements that offers the most efficient physical motion.
ROLLS	Sustaining sound – There are three primary types of rolls in percussion performance: single stroke roll, concert roll, and open roll.

COMPARISON OF COMMON ELEMENTS

PERCUSSION	to	WINDS/STRINGS
Posture	⟷	Posture
Grip	⟷	Embouchure Bow Grip/Hand Position
Striking Motion	⟷	Articulation Bowing Techniques
Dynamics/Volume	⟷	Dynamics/Volume
Sticking	⟷	Fingering/Articulation Bowing
Rolls/Sustained Sounds	⟷	Breath Control Sustain

Percussion performance can be reduced to six *Common Elements.*

POSTURE

Posture is the physical relationship between the performer and the instrument. It includes the general position (baseline) of the body or one of its parts, the playing area, physical adjustments a performer makes to the height of an instrument, and the distance between the performer and an instrument. When determining the correct posture, consider the following items in order:

1. **Baseline**
   Baseline refers to the relaxed, natural position of the body. Determine the baseline position by simply walking in a free, unencumbered manner, as if going for a stroll in the park. Always establish the body's natural baseline posture before playing an instrument. Keep the head up.

2. **Playing Area**
   Playing area refers to the area on any percussion instrument which, when struck, produces the most characteristic (resonant) sound. For example, a snare drum should be played slightly off center; timpani should be played at the point between the edge and center that produces the most resonant sound, and so on. The playing area must be determined before considering other factors of posture.

3. **Height**
   Height refers to the height of an instrument and the adjustments made to the instrument in order to accommodate the body's natural baseline position. Always adjust the height of the instrument to the performer. Avoid contorting the body in an effort to accommodate the height of the instrument. In general, correct height is determined by following the procedure below:

   Proper Playing Position
   1. Stand straight with arms relaxed at side of body.
   2. Bend arms at the elbows until the forearms are parallel to the floor. Keep the upper arms in line with the body.
   3. Drop arms from the elbow approximately 2 to 3 inches.
   4. Relax the wrist and allow the fingers to point toward the floor.
   5. The instrument should be adjusted to touch the fingertips as they appear in Step. 4.

4. **Distance**
   Distance refers to the space between the body and the instrument. In general, correct distance from an instrument is determined by following the procedure below:

   Proper Playing Position
   1. While holding sticks or mallets, stand away from the instrument with arms relaxed at the sides of the body.
   2. Bend arms at the elbows until the forearms are parallel to the floor. Keep the upper arms in line with the body.
   3. Drop arms from the elbows approximately 2 to 3 inches.
   4. Walk forward until the head of the stick or mallet is over the correct playing area.
      Avoid moving the arms forward or backward when approaching the instrument.

GRIP

Refer to "GRIP" in Chapter 3 for a detailed description

MATCHED GRIP is recommended for all percussion performance.

Matched grip is recommended for the following reasons:

1. Matched grip will transfer to all percussion instruments including timpani, keyboard percussion, snare drum, accessory percussion instruments, and drum set.
2. The same muscles are used in each hand, increasing the probability of producing an even, matched sound.
3. Matched grip has more potential power to help control the action or movement.
4. Matched grip will aid in more sustained endurance.
5. Both sticks are held in a like manner.

Matched Grip – Top View

STRIKING MOTION

The manner in which a percussionist strikes an instrument determines the quality of sound produced. PISTON MOTION will provide the most efficient movement for ALL percussion instruments.

Piston Motion is a single motion that starts and ends at a predetermined height.

This height is determined by dynamic level (see page 7). Follow the illustration below for achieving Piston Motion.

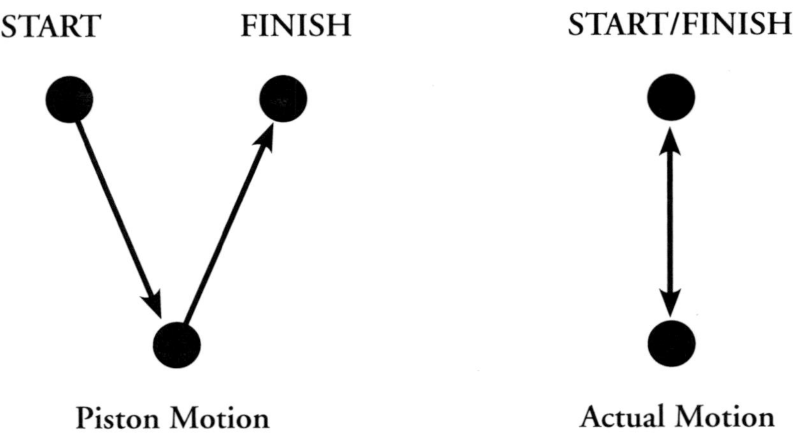

The V shape of this movement as illustrated above does not indicate a glancing blow to the instrument. It represents a single motion in which the stick travels from a predetermined height down to the instrument and returns (up) to the original position. Keep the following points in mind when developing Piston Motion.

1. There is a correct starting height for every dynamic level.
2. Choose the lowest height that preserves a natural, smooth acceleration of sticks.
3. Always prepare for the next motion in advance. The ending position for one motion will be the starting position for the next motion.
4. If the starting point is too low, the motion will feel pinched and tense.
5. If the starting point is too high, it will feel cushioned and restrained.
6. Advanced preparation with Piston Motion is effective for all tempos.
7. The stick should always come to rest at the highest point of the motion.
8. Think one continuous motion, rather than two or more up and down movements.
9. All Piston Motions return to the same level as they started unless the dynamic changes.
10. Avoid wasted motion.

VOLUME

Obtaining the appropriate dynamic level on percussion instruments is directly related to the correct striking motion. Volume is related to stick height – a high motion will produce a loud sound and a motion close to the striking surface will produce a soft sound. Always prepare the stick height of the next sound in advance.

FORMULA:

Loud Volume = High Stick

Soft Volume = Low Stick

In the following illustration, the height of the stick represents preparation of the **NEXT** note or dynamic.

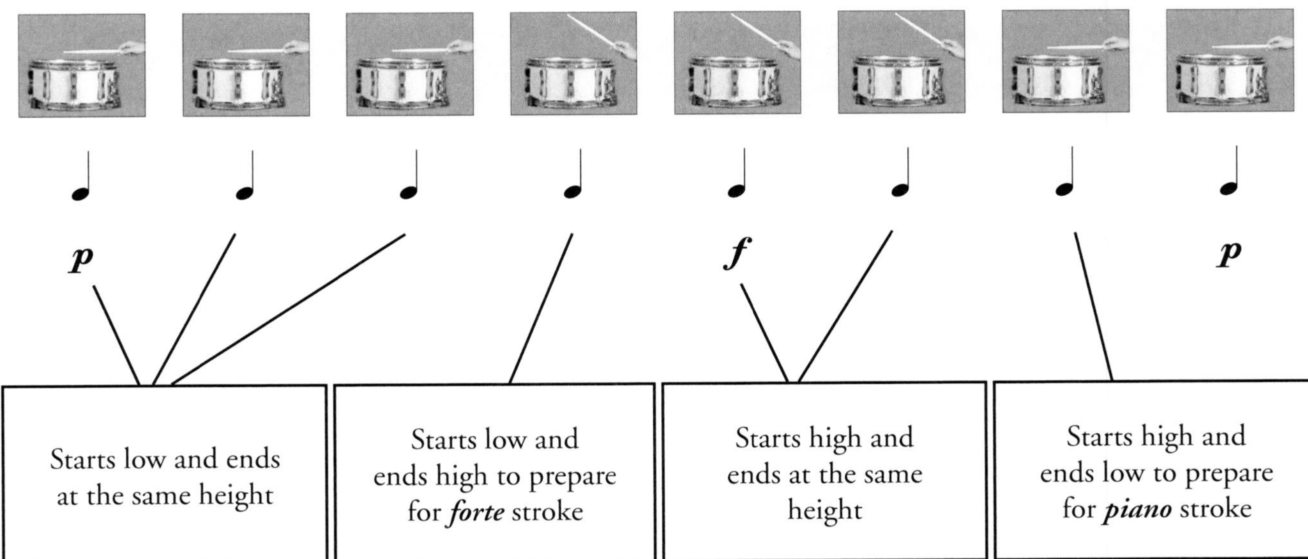

STICKING

The term ***sticking*** refers to the choice of right and/or left hand patterns that provide the most efficient means of achieving a desired musical result. A player's choice of sticking will determine how well a rhythmic passage is performed. The best sticking is determined by the desired musical effect.

Monitoring a percussionist's sticking at the early stages of development is very important. It is easy for a young student to develop habits that will cause permanent problems.

Keep in mind that:

- **A percussionist must be able to perform equally well with both hands.**
- **Rhythmic patterns should be practiced with a variety of stickings.**
- **Young players have a tendency to favor their strong hand.**
  Avoid this tendency. If allowed to progress, they will start most rhythmic figures with the strong hand and start and end rolls with the strong hand. If this tendency is allowed to develop without giving equal attention to the weak hand, irreparable damage will result.

There are three generally recognized sticking systems: the **alternating system**, the **weak hand system**, and the **multiple-line system**. Many refer to the weak hand system as the "lead" system (or right hand lead). For purposes of developing stronger players, the author chooses to apply the technique to the weak hand, thus enhancing overall playing ability. Each system has advantages and disadvantages in various musical settings.

1. ALTERNATING STICKING

The ***alternating sticking system*** advocates a hand-to-hand approach to sticking. That is, if one begins playing with the left hand, then the right hand should follow and vice versa. There is a strict alternation of hands. This type of "sticking" helps young percussionists develop the ability to use each hand equally well. Alternating sticking should be emphasized until the student is comfortable playing any figure with either hand.

Advantages

1. Gives equal responsibility to both hands.
2. Easily transfers to all other percussion instruments.
3. Recommended for fast passages.
4. Recommended for students who are partial to lead systems.

The **alternating sticking system** is recommended for beginning percussionists because it helps develop the ability to use each hand equally well.

2. WEAK HAND STICKING

The ***weak hand sticking system*** suggests that all primary pulses, principal beats, and strong accents are played with the "weak" hand and the remaining beats, up beats, and embellished notes are played with the other hand. Pick-ups with one or three notes start with the "strong" hand, two- or four-note pick-ups begin with the weak hand. Most rolls begin on the weak hand. The weak hand system is a structured system. If learned thoroughly, it may aid in sight-reading certain musical figures within a fairly narrow range of tempi.

Many refer to this sticking system as the "lead" system or the "right hand lead" system. For purposes of developing stronger players, the author chooses to apply the technique to the weak hand, thus enhancing overall playing ability.

EXAMPLES OF THE WEAK HAND STICKING SYSTEM

(assuming that the left hand is the weak hand)

STICKING (cont.)

3. MULTIPLE-LINE STICKING

The following rules for determining the appropriate sticking for multiple-line parts should be applied to timpani, keyboard percussion (marimba, bells, vibraphone, etc.), and multiple percussion performance.

RULES OF MULTIPLE-LINE PLAYING

Step-By-Step

1. Arrange instruments according to pitch … lowest on the left … highest on the right.

2. Try alternating sticking first.

3. If alternating sticking is inappropriate, apply the parameters of time and distance to determine double-sticking (two notes with the same hand).
   Time – Use the double-sticking that affords the most time to prepare.
   Distance – Use the double-sticking that requires the least distance to travel.

4. The simplest sticking is usually the best.

5. Avoid cross-sticking, triple sticking, and lead sticking unless absolutely necessary.

6. **RULE:** With an **odd** numbered group of notes on the same pitch, begin with **outside** hand.
   With an **even** numbered group of notes on the same pitch, begin with **inside** hand.

   Inside Hand = hand closest to next note
   Outside Hand = hand farthest from next note

As noted above, all percussionists should begin with the alternating sticking system, and it should be emphasized until the student can use both hands equally well. When this is achieved, introduce sticking patterns that challenge students and help develop more flexibility. Private lessons may be necessary in order to closely monitor students' progress.

No source exists that guides percussionists through a logical sequence of sticking systems. Until such a source becomes available, it will be the teacher's responsibility to carefully monitor this aspect of percussionists' training.

ROLLS

(Sustaining Sound)

Roll Notation:

THREE TYPES OF ROLLS

1. **Single Stroke Roll:**

A succession of alternating single strokes in which the stick strikes the playing surface once per motion.

This type of roll is most commonly used on timpani and keyboard percussion.

2. **Concert Roll:**
Also called Multiple Bounce or Buzz Roll

A succession of alternating single strokes in which the stick strikes the playing surface multiple times per motion.

This type of roll is most commonly used on snare drum.

3. **Open Roll:**
Also called Rudimental Roll

A succession of alternating single strokes in which the stick strikes the playing surface two times per motion.

This type of roll is most commonly used on snare drum, but has direct application to most percussion instruments when sticks or mallets are used and quick double motions are required.

Chapter 2

HOW TO DEVELOP A PERCUSSION SECTION

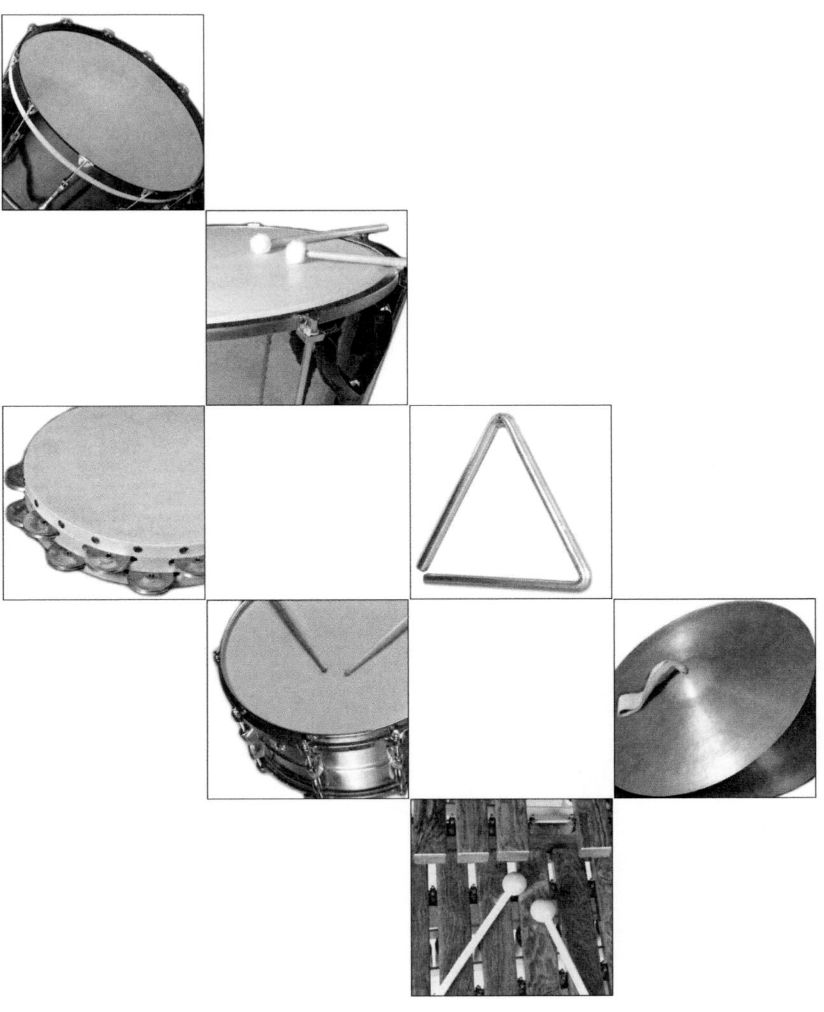

Chapter 2

HOW TO DEVELOP A PERCUSSION SECTION

The development of an outstanding percussion section in a school band or orchestra is dependent upon the director's attitude toward percussion, the director's knowledge of percussion performance, and the students' involvement in the kinds of activities that enhance performance skills and attitude.

> The director's knowledge of percussion performance, the director's attitude toward percussion, and the students' involvement in activities are the keys to the development of an outstanding percussion section.

Percussionists will develop adequate performance techniques, a keen sense of musicianship, and a positive attitude if they participate in appropriate activities.

Well-trained percussionists will actively participate, on a regular basis, in four activities:

- Warm-up with band/orchestra
- Playing percussion parts in band/orchestra
- Percussion ensemble
- Private instruction

Each activity needs to be carefully monitored by an interested, knowledgeable teacher. Keep in mind that each of these activities is essential in the development of contemporary percussionists. Excluding one or more activity will reduce a student's rate of success.

WARM-UP WITH THE BAND/ORCHESTRA

Warming up is important for all musicians, including percussionists. They should be contributing members of an ensemble during all phases of a rehearsal. The development of good tone quality, flexibility, intonation, balance, and nuance is as important for percussionists as it is for trumpet and clarinet players. An interesting and challenging percussion warm-up with the full ensemble provides an ideal opportunity to develop those skills.

GUIDELINES FOR WARM-UP WITH THE BAND/ORCHESTRA

1. Develop a ***rotating*** schedule (See WARM-UP SCHEDULE on the next page), assigning each player to a specific instrument during full ensemble warm-up.

2. Since, percussionists need to learn to play several instruments, provide opportunities to perform on all basic percussion instruments – snare drum, timpani, keyboard percussion, and accessory instruments during warm-up.

3. Post warm-up assignments in an area easily seen by the section.

SAMPLE WARM-UP SCHEDULE

(Change this schedule weekly or monthly)

	LARRY	MIKE	SCOTT	PAM	JOHN	SUE
Monday	xylo	marimba or vibes	snare	timpani	snare	accessory
Tuesday	xylo	marimba or vibes	snare	timpani	snare	accessory
Wednesday	snare	snare	xylo	marimba or vibes	accessory	timpani
Thursday	snare	snare	xylo	marimba or vibes	accessory	timpani
Friday	accessory	timpani	snare	snare	xylo	xylo

4. The goal is to have everyone playing during warm-up. All clarinet and trumpet players participate in warm-ups. The same should be true for all percussionists.

5. The percussion warm-up must be organized. That is, each player must have specifically assigned rhythm, pattern, etc. for each warm-up etude, exercise, or scale (See PATTERNS for PERCUSSION DURING FULL BAND WARM-UP on the next page). Improvising should not be allowed in this setting.

In the following examples on page 16:

- The band plays a B-flat major scale.
- The director will select and assign a pattern or patterns in advance for the percussionists.
  - Non-pitched percussion (snare drum, cymbals, bass drum, tambourine, etc.) will select from Patterns 1-6.
  - Keyboard percussion (9-11) and timpani (7-8) will also have a number of choices from which to select (see next page).

The following example illustrates one possible scenario where snare drum plays #1 with LLRR sticking, tambourine plays #3 with a thumb roll, crash cymbals play #2, bass drum plays #6, timpani plays #7, and keyboard percussion plays #10.

PATTERNS FOR PERCUSSION DURING FULL BAND WARM-UP

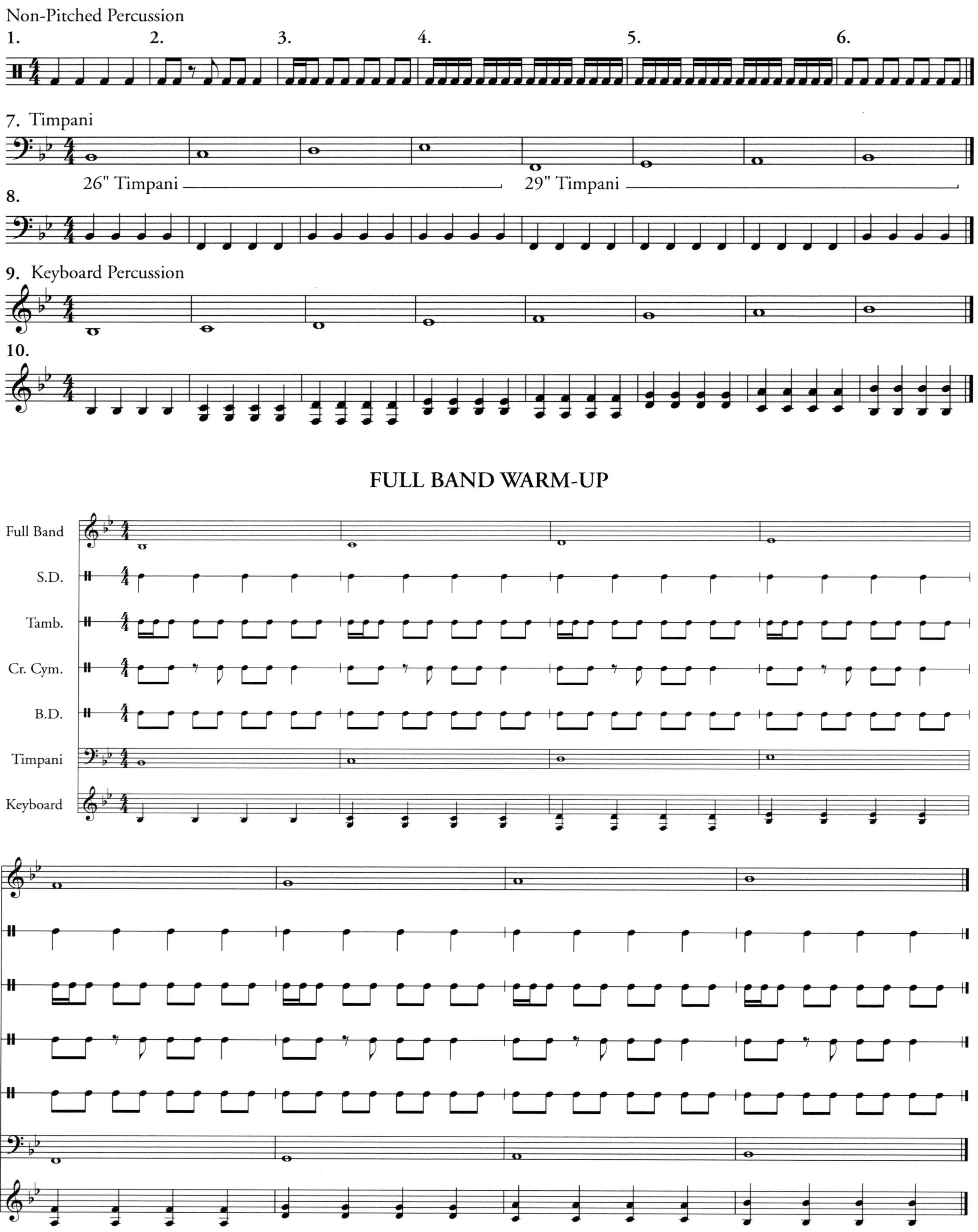

GUIDELINES FOR WARM-UP WITH THE BAND/ORCHESTRA (cont.)

6. Insist that percussionists blend and balance with other instruments. A common complaint about having percussionists warm up with the rest of ensemble is that it becomes difficult for the director and other musicians to listen for balance and intonation. If a director cannot hear the rest of the ensemble, he/she may need to assess his/her expectations of percussion during warm-up (i.e which patterns are being played). Are the percussionists playing too loudly? If a director cannot hear the ensemble properly when percussionists are included in the warm-up, then one could assume that it is impossible to play in tune while rehearsing or performing a piece by David Gillingham or Richard Strauss. Percussionists are part of the ensemble and they must participate in the same kinds of activities that help other musicians develop their sense of musicianship. Remember, one should expect the same degree of musicianship from a percussionist that one expects from a first chair clarinet player.

7. If percussionists develop listening skills during warm-ups, the likelihood of transferring those skills to performance situations is significantly increased.

8. Use the warm-up to develop specific technical/musical skills, such as articulation, dynamic control, tuning, scales, key signatures, embellishments, etc. Always have specific goals in mind for each rehearsal and develop etudes and exercises that complement these goals.

9. Warming up with the band or orchestra may be the only time that percussionists work on the technical and musical aspects of their playing in an organized fashion. Five to ten minutes a day will work wonders for young percussionists.

10. Since no class warm-up book exists that treats percussion in a comprehensive way, the director will need to write exercises and etudes that are appropriate for their students. These exercises should be cumulative in that they should progress from fairly simple to highly complex in order to allow students to gradually obtain necessary skills. Furthermore, the exercises should take into account specific performance techniques for each percussion instrument so that they aid in building and maintaining good playing habits. Start with simple rhythmic patterns and systematically increase complexity.

SIMPLE TO COMPLEX RHYTHMIC PATTERNS FOR WARM-UP

NOTE: Avoid the following non-productive alternatives to having percussionists warm up with the band or orchestra.

1. Require percussionists to sit quietly and listen to other musicians warm up.

2. Require percussionists to file music or move equipment for the drama teacher.

3. Have percussionists attend study hall until the wind and brass players are ready to rehearse the music.

PLAYING PERCUSSION PARTS IN BAND/ORCHESTRA

If one were to ask a percussionist what it is like to play in a band or orchestra, they would likely answer resoundingly, "Boring". After all, consider what percussionists do during ensemble rehearsals; sit for extended periods with nothing to perform; play occasionally; or worse, never play at all. Percussionists often complain of never getting to play important parts or of having to fight upperclassmen for even the smallest part. Once a student has a part, it may be one that allows for little musical growth and development.

It is easy to say, "That is the way it is; you should get accustomed to sitting idle and counting rests for long periods of time." In a professional setting, this is undoubtedly true; but the role of a band and orchestra director is to develop young musicians to their fullest capacity by providing meaningful activities. Percussionists need to play all basic percussion instruments as often as possible. There should be no such thing as a student that plays only bass drum, or snare drum, or timpani.

The suggestions below will assist conductors with providing a positive experience for young percussionists during a typical rehearsal.

GUIDELINES FOR THE PERCUSSION SECTION DURING REHEARSAL

1. Get as many percussionists involved as possible by ***doubling parts*** where appropriate. If a director demands the ultimate musicianship from each player, volume and precision is easily controlled.

2. ***Add keyboard percussion parts*** by doubling woodwind or brass instruments, or write original parts for keyboard percussion. This is an unexplored area with tremendous potential for brave composers interested in developing better percussionists.

3. ***Add accessory parts*** that complement the nature of the music being played. No composition is so sacred that directors should require the majority of the percussion section to sit idly while a select few play.

4. Percussionists need to learn to play several instruments. Provide them with opportunities to ***perform on all basic percussion instruments*** during rehearsals, such as snare drum, timpani, keyboard percussion, and accessory instruments.

5. ***Develop a rotating schedule*** (See PERCUSSION ASSIGNMENT CHART on next page), and assign each player to a specific instrument for each composition.

SAMPLE PERCUSSION ASSIGNMENT CHART

	Composition 1	Composition 2	Composition 3	Composition 4
Larry	Snare Drum	Timpani	Bells	Crash Cymbals
Pam	Bass Drum	Marimba	Snare Drum	Tambourine
Mike	Xylophone	Snare Drum	Timpani	Woodblock
Sue	Crash Cymbals	Bass Drum	Vibraphone	Timpani
John	Timpani	Crash Cymbals	Bass Drum	Xylophone
Scott	Triangle	Bells	Crash Cymbals	Snare Drum

6. ***Post the instrument assignments*** in an area easily seen by all percussionists.

7. When instruction or criticism is appropriate, approach the issue with a ***step-by-step approach***, so students have a definite procedure to apply to similar situations.

8. ***Allow time between compositions*** for percussionists to change the arrangement of instruments. Show them a method for making set-up changes as efficiently as possible.

9. Each percussionist should get into the habit of putting the percussion area in order before rehearsal begins. Set-up can be a simple procedure if you assign each percussionist a specific job (See SET-UP ASSIGNMENTS on the next page). Place a list of these jobs on a chart and post it in an obvious place near the rehearsal area so everyone in the section can see it. Each individual should fulfill his/her set-up assignment before rehearsal begins, then return the same item(s) to its original location after rehearsal. ***Use the same percussion set-up every day*** so that all of the musicians in the ensemble develop a sense of organization and neatness.

10. Ask other students to stay away from the percussion area before and after rehearsal so percussionists have a chance to efficiently operate in their own environment. It is difficult to maneuver when objects (like horn cases) are constantly in the way or when percussion instruments are used as tables.

11. In order to give young percussionists the best possible education, directors must develop a keen understanding of the musical potential and technical demands of percussion instruments.

12. If every wind player has ***his/her own music folder***, do the same for percussionists. Mark music folders by instrument name or individual student name. Always have a copy of music for every percussionist. Never allow two or more percussionists to read from the same copy or the same music stand.

13. ***Provide padded music stands or tables*** and require percussionists to keep their mallets, small instruments, and other potential noisemakers on the padded surface. When a percussionist is not playing, his/her sticks/mallets should be placed on the padded surface.

SAMPLE SET-UP ASSIGNMENTS

Larry	Bass Drum, Bass Drum Cover, BD Mallets, Mallet Stand for BD
Mike	Timpani, Timpani Covers, Mallet Stand for Timpani, Timpani Throne
Pam	Snare Drum and Stand, Music Stands for All Instruments, Unlock and Lock Cabinets
Scott	Crash Cymbals, Suspended Cymbal and Stand, Mallet Stand for SD and Sus. Cym.
Sue	Keyboard Covers, Clean Keyboard Instruments, Mallet Stands for Keyboard Instruments
John	Accessories, Table for Cymbals and Accessories

PERCUSSION ENSEMBLE

Playing the parts in most band and orchestra pieces is not enough to develop percussionists to their fullest potential. Just as small ensembles (quartets, quintets) aid in the development of clarinet, trumpet, and flute players, percussion ensemble provides an opportunity for percussionists to develop skills that would go unattended otherwise or develop at a much slower pace. In fact, wind and string players will usually obtain more of the necessary skills in a large ensemble than percussionists, because wind and strings players are always involved in the kinds of musical activities that develop sensitivity and musical awareness (scales, articulation, tuning, etc.).

Active participation in a well-organized percussion ensemble will:

- Improve percussionists' ability to play in larger groups.
- Promote a sense of musicianship beyond that required in other literature.
- Elevate performance to a principal role rather than one of support in other types of literature.
- Provide an opportunity to introduce percussionists to a wider variety of performance techniques.

GUIDELINES FOR PERCUSSION ENSEMBLE

1. ***Schedule regular rehearsals.*** Percussion ensemble must be an ongoing activity with regularly scheduled rehearsals. Anything less will result in frustration.

2. ***Post the rehearsal order*** before rehearsal begins to avoid wasting time.

3. ***Allow time for set-up.*** Remember that each composition will likely have a different set-up. Show students effective ways to organize instruments to minimize wasted time.

4. Take time to ***illustrate proper playing techniques*** and insist that each percussionist plays with good form.

5. Insist that ***everyone participates in setting up*** the instruments and returning them to their designated storage area.

6. A ***qualified teacher*** should direct the percussion ensemble, not a student.

7. ***Schedule a performance*** of the percussion ensemble. The ensemble might present its own recital/concert or it might be featured on a band concert. If the ensemble is a part of a larger instrumental concert, give the percussionists time to set up.

8. ***Require all percussionists to participate*** in percussion ensemble. Otherwise, some will develop adequate performance skills and others will not, causing a large dichotomy in the percussion section.

9. ***Play challenging literature*** that involves a wide variety of pitched and non-pitched percussion instruments.

10. Give percussionists the experience and satisfaction of ***playing a keyboard percussion part.*** Do not recruit pianists and flute players to do what percussionists should be doing.

PRIVATE INSTRUCTION

Private instruction is an essential ingredient in the development of all musicians. It is especially important for percussionists given the number of instruments to learn. Individualized instruction on an ongoing basis provides an opportunity for musicians to develop beyond what is considered the norm – the kind of limited instruction often possible in group situations. While the benefits of private instruction are obvious, teachers will be wise to develop their program of study so that students will have ample opportunity to develop without it.

GUIDELINES FOR PRIVATE INSTRUCTION

1. The teacher must have a solid pedagogical philosophy. Not all "drummers" are good percussion teachers.

2. Private instruction should be continuous. Intermittent lessons are less effective than long-term study.

3. Although a teacher who is also a percussionist is desirable, he/she need not be a percussionist if he/she understands the ***Common Elements*** of percussion performance and has a supreme command of musicianship.

4. Private instruction should be broad-based; instruction should include technical as well as musical development.

5. Instruction should include study on pitched as well as non-pitched instruments.

6. For young percussionists, avoid teachers that teach only drum set and/or snare drum and exclude other percussion instruments.

MANAGING THE PERCUSSION SECTION

Percussionists sometimes act as if they were in a world of their own. Isolated at the back of the room, they face difficulties - and temptations - unlike those of other musicians. It is possible, though, to guide percussionists to high standards of musicianship and to guide them away from disruptive behavior that might occur if left unattended. Devising a plan for percussionists to follow as they set up, warm up, rehearse, and depart takes time; but the results are gratifying. Once a system is established that deals effectively with each of the four parts of a rehearsal, percussionists will accept no less.

FOUR PARTS OF A REHEARSAL
Arrival/Set-Up
Warm-Up
Rehearsal
Pack-Up/Departure

ARRIVAL/SET-UP

Each percussionist should develop the habit of putting the percussion area in order before rehearsal begins. Set-up can be a simple procedure if each percussionist is assigned a specific task (See SET-UP ASSIGNMENTS p. 20). Place a list of these jobs on a chart and post it in an obvious place near the rehearsal area so everyone in the section can see it. Each individual should fulfill his/her set-up assignment before the rehearsal begins, then return the same item(s) to its original location after rehearsal. Use the same basic percussion set-up every day so that all of the musicians in the ensemble develop a sense of organization and neatness. The set-up should account for expansion if the literature requires additional instruments. SEE BELOW.

Possible Percussion Set-Up in Band or Orchestra

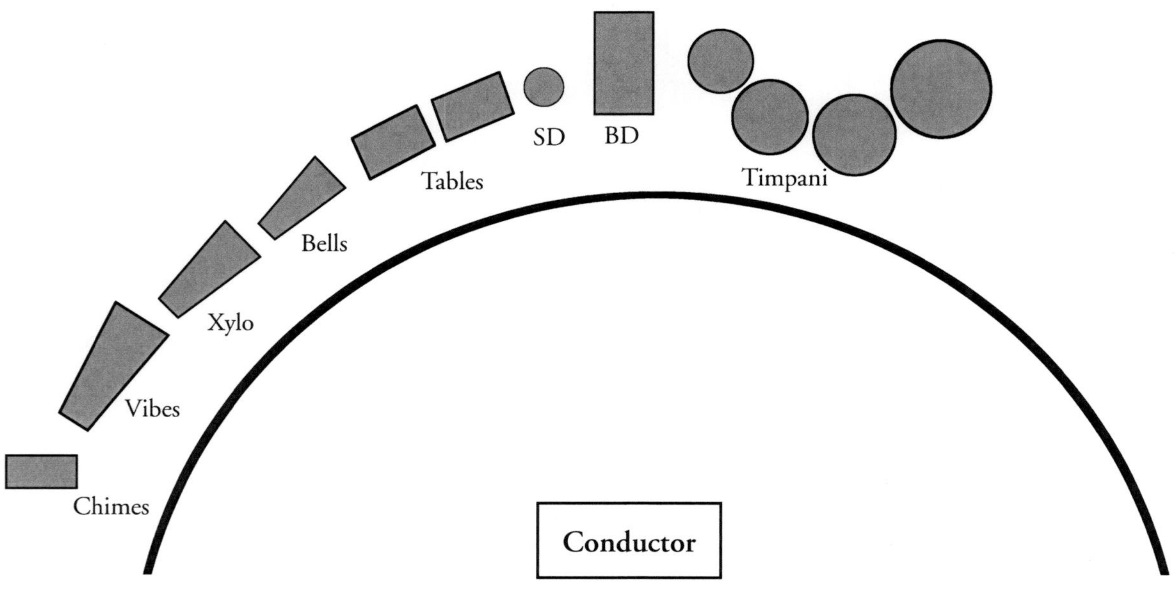

WARM-UP

Refer to Warm-Up with the Band/Orchestra (page 14)

REHEARSAL

Refer to Playing Percussion Parts in Band/Orchestra (page 18)

PACK-UP/DEPARTURE

At the end of every rehearsal, students should return the percussion area to its original appearance. The students responsible for set-up at the beginning of rehearsal should return all instruments and equipment to the storage cabinets and drawers, being sure to lock them.

Allow time for percussionists to put equipment away in a neat and orderly fashion. If a director continues rehearsal until after the bell rings, expect to find instruments and accessories dropped in a corner or improperly stored. With practice, it takes about two minutes for everyone to replace items and fulfill their responsibilities.

By organizing the percussion section in a systematic way, directors will take the first step toward ensuring that young percussionists will develop as first-rate musicians. Dividing the rehearsal into four segments and planning goals for each one is just the start of developing percussionists' musicianship fully.

A good percussion section will:

- Have a highly sophisticated plan for ***organizing their space.***
- ***Participate in daily warm-up*** with the entire ensemble and play (on a rotating basis) all basic percussion instruments during warm-up.
- Demonstrate ***competence on all basic percussion instruments*** (snare drum, timpani, keyboard percussion, bass drum, cymbals, tambourine, triangle)
- Participate, on a regular basis, in a ***percussion ensemble.***
- Demonstrate the same, or higher, degree of ***musical sensitivity*** as other musicians.
- ***Play on good quality equipment*** and keep the equipment in good condition.

MARCHING PERCUSSION

Marching percussion is often considered an area of specialty within percussion pedagogy. However, the wise teacher will approach concert percussion and marching percussion as more similar than different. The primary difference between concert percussion and marching percussion is in the recognition that concert percussion does not involve carrying an instrument, while drum line may require (but not always) a percussionist to carry an instrument. Although marching percussion may involve visual effects, the inherent playing techniques for both types of performance (concert and marching) should be based on the same information. One approach to marching percussion requires players to perform with a very stiff and rigid style. This type of playing style will not transfer to concert situations and may cause problems that young players may never overcome. A pedagogical approach based on the **Common Elements** will provide the best approach for developing musicianship and technique in young percussionists.

There is a tendency to assume that concert percussion and marching percussion are different; that marching requires different techniques, different styles, and a different pedagogical approach. Keep in mind that the function of the instruments may differ among the various styles, but playing techniques and the concept of tone quality should remain the same. Work toward developing long-term playing habits. Since the field of marching percussion evolves so quickly, any attempt to deal with it in this text would be soon out of date. Ask your instructor to recommend one of the many resources available dealing with marching percussion.

PREVENTIVE MAINTENANCE OF PERCUSSION INSTRUMENTS

If proper care is taken of percussion instruments, repair costs will be significantly lowered and the life of each instrument will be greatly prolonged. Below is a general guide to the proper storage and handling of percussion instruments.

STORAGE OF PERCUSSION INSTRUMENTS

Percussion instruments must be stored in an area specifically designated to and designed for percussion instrument storage. Improper storage is perhaps the single most significant factor in an instrument's premature deterioration.

1. **Large instruments** (timpani, bass drum, keyboard instruments): Cover and keep in a low-traffic area.

2. **All other instruments** (snare drums, bongos, toms, cymbals, etc.): Lay flat on a padded shelf in a locked cabinet.

3. **Sticks and mallets** should be stored in a dry, secure place.

HANDLING OF PERCUSSION INSTRUMENTS

1. Never place books, bags, instrument cases, or food on any percussion instrument at any time, whether the instrument is covered or not.

2. Never lean or sit on any percussion instrument.

3. Strike percussion instruments only with the mallets specifically designed for use on that type of instrument. Playing with mallets that are too hard or made from unsuitable material can cause irreparable damage.

4. When moving percussion instruments, lift them across rough surfaces and over harsh bumps, such as doorjambs and sidewalk seams. Always avoid dragging the pedal across the ground when moving timpani, vibraphones, and chimes. Always move instruments by the frame or braces, never by a part of the instrument that would affect its quality of sound.

5. Sticks and mallets should be placed on a padded stand in a performance situation. Never place mallets on the floor.

6. When to replace drum heads:
   - If there is a puncture, cut, or tear in head
   - If there is excessive wear on the head:
     - Textured or coated head is worn smooth over most of its surface
     - Great number of stick marks and dents on its head
     - Opaque or coated heads have a mottled or pock-marked appearance
   - Broken tambourine head (Tambourine head repair kits are available from companies such as Grover Pro Percussion Products and Black Swamp. Simple instructions are included

STUDENT PURCHASE GUIDE

Percussionists should make the same financial investment as other instrumentalists. The following is a guide that students might use when making stick, mallet, and accessory purchases. The equipment need not be purchased at the outset, but gradually, as performance competencies and desire demands. Inform beginning percussionists of their responsibilities in terms of instrument and accessory purchase.

All percussionists should own the items on the list below by the time they enter high school.

Snare Drum Sticks

1 Pair General Purpose (Concert)
1 Pair General Purpose (Drum Set)
1 Pair General Purpose (Marching Band)

Timpani Mallets

1 Pair Normal Staccato
1 Pair Ultra Staccato

Keyboard Percussion Mallets

1 Pair Hard Plastic (Bells)
1 Pair Medium Plastic (Xylophone)
2 Pairs Medium Yarn (4-Mallet Marimba, Cymbals, Multiple Percussion)
1 Pair Hard Yarn (Marimba, Cymbals, Multiple Percussion)
1 Pair Medium Rubber (Woodblock, Xylophone, Multiple Percussion)

Mallet Case or Bag

Pitch Pipe

Wire Brushes

Metronome

Triangle

6" Triangle
Triangle Clip
3 Pairs of Beaters (thin, medium, thick)

Tambourine

10" Double Row Jingle
Skin Head

Chapter 3

SNARE DRUM

Chapter 3

SNARE DRUM

The Common Elements

Posture
Grip
Striking Motion
Volume
Sticking
Rolls

WHY BEGINNERS START ON SNARE DRUM

The snare drum is usually the first instrument introduced to beginning students. Historically, beginners started on snare drum because it was the only instrument in the percussion family having significant solo repertoire, and because it was the primary instrument of marching percussion sections. The best players usually played the snare drum since those parts were the most difficult.

While snare drum remains an important part of percussion study, it is no longer the only instrument in the percussion family with significant repertoire, nor is it the center of attention in marching band, concert band, orchestra, or percussion ensemble. Snare drum study provides a logical beginning, since many snare drum techniques transfer to other percussion instruments. Physical movements, notation, etc. required for snare drum performance are essential for all percussionists. However, it should be noted that beginning percussionists should devote an equal amount of time learning keyboard percussion and skills that will transfer to timpani.

Snare drum provides a logical beginning since many snare drum techniques **transfer** to other percussion instruments.

However, in the hands of a good teacher, young percussionists should be able to start on ANY percussion instrument.

MINIMUM SNARE DRUM SKILLS FOR HIGH SCHOOL GRADUATES

	Student Names			
1. Demonstrate good posture while playing, including height of the instrument, distance between the instrument and the player, and general body position.				
2. Demonstrate working knowledge of the correct playing area.				
3. Demonstrate correct matched grip.				
4. Demonstrate piston motion.				
5. Demonstrate use of stick height to attain desired dynamic level.				
6. Demonstrate a working knowledge of how to determine appropriate sticking.				
7. Demonstrate open and closed rolls using tempo and dynamics as indicators of appropriate roll base.				
8. Perform flams, drags, and ruffs correctly in a musical context.				
9. Demonstrate proper care and maintenance of the instrument, including working knowledge of how to change a snare drum head.				

POSTURE

There are four factors that determine good posture on snare drum.

1. Baseline
2. Height of Drum
3. Playing Area
4. Distance of Drum from Body

BASELINE

Baseline refers to the relaxed, natural position of the body. Determine the baseline position by simply walking in a free, unencumbered manner, as if going for an evening stroll in the park. Always establish the body's natural baseline posture before playing an instrument. Keep the head up.

HEIGHT OF SNARE DRUM

Follow the procedure below for determining the correct height of the snare drum. This procedure will insure correct posture by accounting for physical differences among individuals.

Step-By-Step

1. Stand straight with arms relaxed at sides.
2. Bend arms at the elbow until the forearms are parallel to the floor, with palms facing the floor.
3. Drop arms from the elbow approximately 2 to 3 inches.
4. Relax the wrist and allow the fingers to point toward the floor.
5. The snare drum should be adjusted to touch the fingers as they appear in Step No. 4.

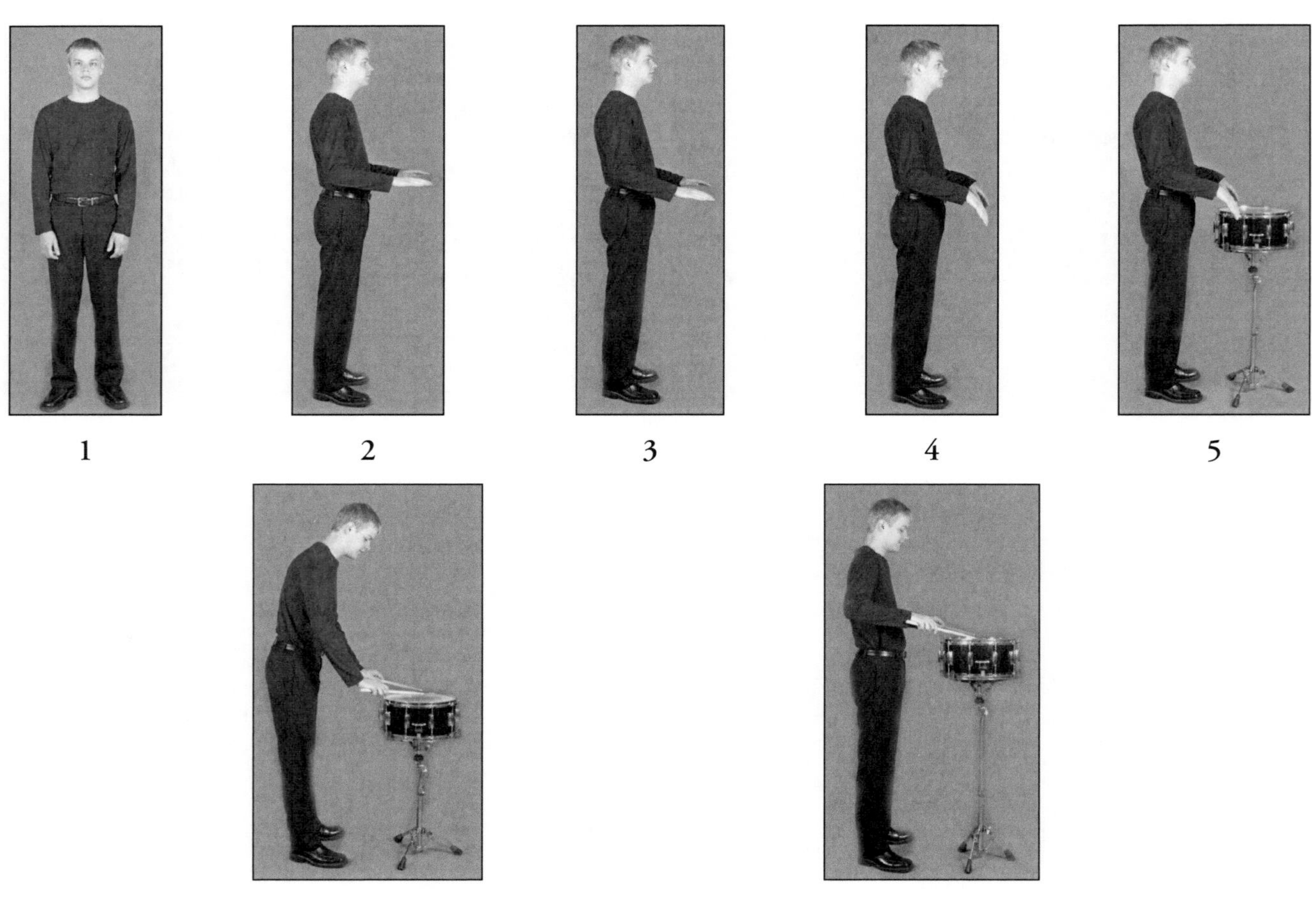

1 2 3 4 5

Drum Too Low **Drum Too High**

PLAYING AREA

Step-By-Step

1. The correct playing area for snare drum is just off center, towards the body.
2. The tips of the sticks should be close together, not separated as in 9 o'clock and 3 o'clock.

Establishing the correct playing area is vital. One must know the correct playing area in order to determine the proper distance of the body from the snare drum.

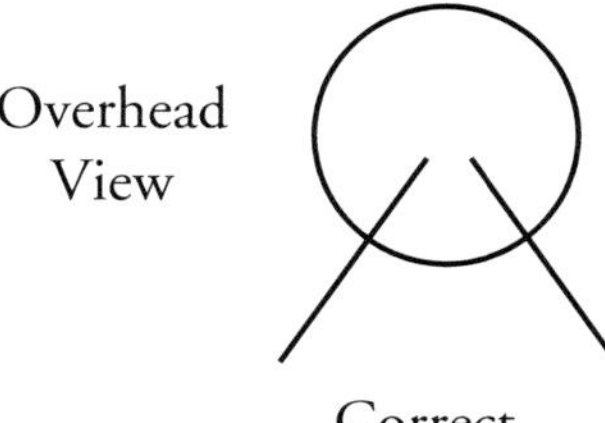

Correct

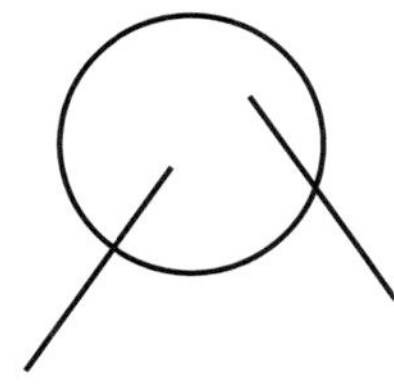
Incorrect

Incorrect

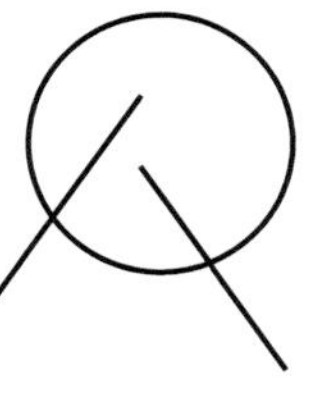
Incorrect

Position of Snare Strainer (See Snare Drum Parts on p. 50)

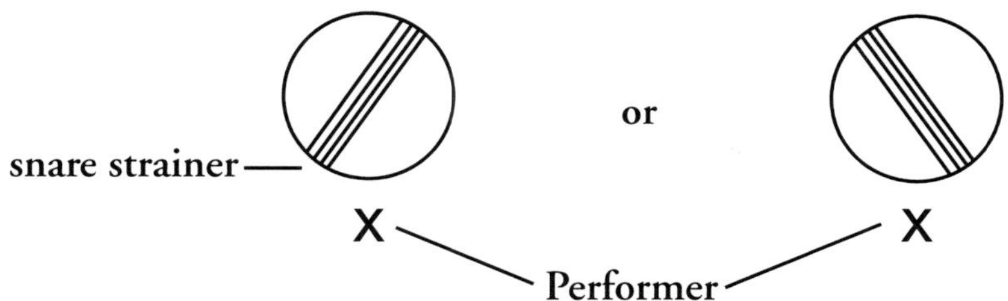

DISTANCE FROM THE SNARE DRUM

Step-By-Step

1. While holding sticks, stand away from the instrument with arms relaxed at the sides of the body.
2. Bend arms at the elbows until the forearms are parallel to the floor. Keep the upper arms in line with the body.
3. Drop arms from the elbows approximately 2 to 3 inches.
4. Walk forward until the head of the stick or mallet is over the correct playing area. Avoid moving the arms forward or backward when approaching the instrument.

Students will often stand too close to the drum causing an uncomfortable playing position. Insist that students practice the procedure above until they feel comfortable when standing the correct distance from the instrument.

Standing Too Close

Standing Too Far Away

CORRECT DISTANCE

GRIP

HOW TO HOLD SNARE DRUM STICKS

TOP VIEW

SIDE VIEW

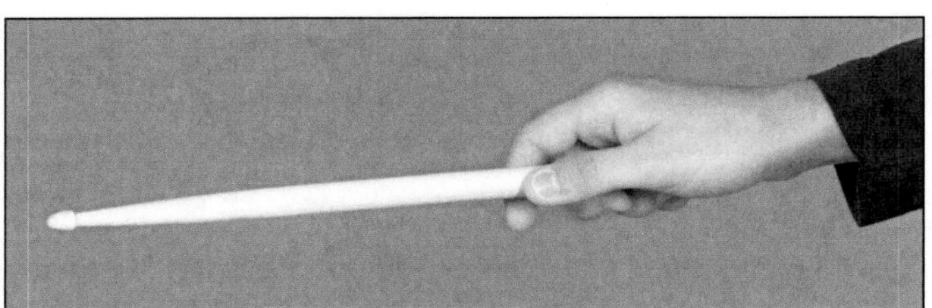

MATCHED GRIP is recommended for all percussion performance. It is recommended for the following reasons:

1. Matched grip will transfer to playing timpani, keyboard percussion, drum set, and all of the accessory percussion instruments.

2. The same muscles are used in each hand increasing the probability of producing an even, matched sound.

3. Matched grip has more potential power to help control the action or movement.

4. Matched grip will produce more sustained endurance.

5. Easy to comprehend.

6. Both sticks are held in like manner.

Matched Grip will transfer to timpani, keyboard percussion, drum set, and accessory instruments.

HOW TO INTRODUCE THE MATCHED GRIP

Since matched grip is very natural, it is easy to learn and will transfer to other percussion instruments. Avoid talking too much about the details of holding the sticks. A simple demonstration of the correct grip will usually be more effective than a lengthy explanation.

Step-By-Step

Method No. 1

1. With the longest finger of each hand, hold the stick by each end (Fig. A).

2. Divide the stick into three equal parts using the thumbs (Fig. B).

3. Grasp the stick where the thumb nearest the butt of the stick touches by placing the index finger directly across from the thumb. The thumb should be flat and the index finger should be placed so that the stick touches the finger between the first and second joint from the end of the finger. Curl the index finger around the stick. The fulcrum is now formed. The fulcrum is the most important factor in obtaining a secure grip. It must be carefully monitored.

4. Gently curl the second finger around the stick without applying pressure. Simply touch the stick with the second finger.

5. The third and fourth (little finger) fingers are curled around the stick but do not necessarily touch it. They provide support and control but do not actually grasp the stick.

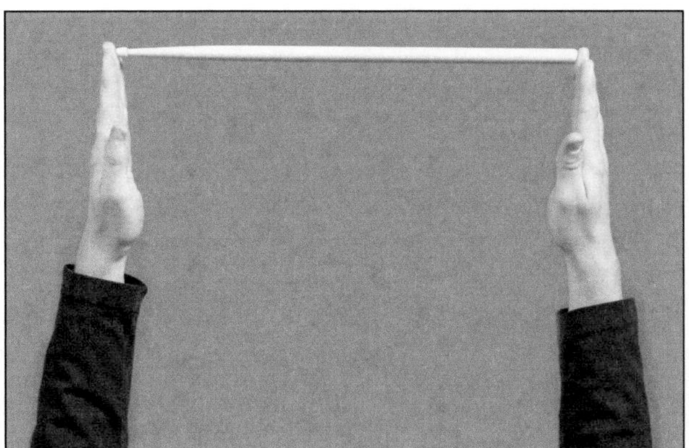

Figure A

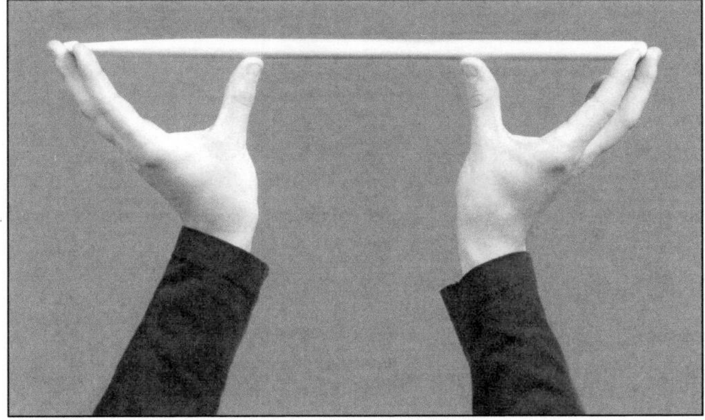

Figure B

Step-By-Step

Method No. 2

1. Lay a snare drum stick on a padded (carpeted) surface.

2. Ask the student to pick up the stick in a very natural way. He will probably do it correctly.

3. Explain that the stick must be held at the point one third of the distance from the butt of the stick.

4. Demonstrate.

GRIP (cont.)

COMMON ISSUES WITH MATCHED GRIP

Be sure that:
- Third and fourth fingers do not extend outward.
- Stick is not held with the third and fourth fingers, displacing the fulcrum.
- First finger does not extend straight out.
- Fulcrum is one third of the distance from butt of stick.
- Thumb does not point downward instead of straight along stick.
- Fulcrum is not formed with second finger instead of index finger.

The grip must be monitored until it becomes firmly established. As new techniques are introduced, one may experience problems with the grip. Students will often try to change the grip (usually unconsciously) in an effort to learn a new technique. It must be constantly monitored in order to avoid developing bad habits. Do not assume that once a student can demonstrate the correct grip it will remain so forever.

TRADITIONAL GRIP
(not recommended)

Another grip, the traditional grip, differs from the matched grip in that it involves an unnatural left hand position. The traditional grip was developed in order to accommodate the slanted drum used in marching. Since drums are no longer carried at an angle, it is no longer necessary to use the traditional grip. Remember, it was developed to accommodate a slanted drum, not because it provided percussionists with greater technical facility.

Slanted Drum with Matched Grip

Slanted Drum with Traditional Grip

Disadvantage of Traditional Grip

1. Involves different muscles in each hand.
2. Will not transfer to other percussion instruments.
3. Difficult to learn. A considerable amount of time is usually spent trying to correct the common maladies associated with this grip.
4. Less likely to produce a matched sound since each hand strikes the drum with a different grip.

STRIKING MOTION

The manner in which a percussionist strikes an instrument determines the quality of sound produced. PISTON MOTION will provide the most efficient movement for ALL percussion instruments.

Piston Motion is a single motion that starts and ends at a predetermined height.

This height is determined by dynamic level (see page 6). Follow the guidelines below for achieving Piston Motion.

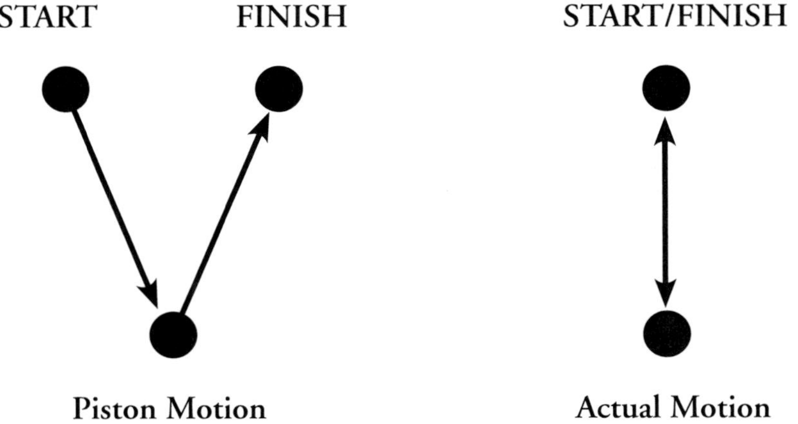

The V shape of this movement as illustrated above does not indicate a glancing blow to the instrument. It represents a single motion in which the stick travels from a predetermined height down to the instrument and returns (up) to the original position. Keep the following points in mind when developing this motion.

1. There is a correct starting height for every dynamic level.
2. Choose the lowest height that preserves a natural, smooth acceleration of sticks.
3. Always prepare for the next motion in advance. The ending position for one motion will be starting position for the next motion.
4. If the starting point is too low, the motion will feel pinched and tense.
5. If the starting point is too high, it will feel cushioned and restrained.
6. It is effective for all tempos.
7. The stick should always come to rest at the highest point of the motion.
8. Think one continuous motion, rather than two or more (up and down) movements.
9. All piston motions return to the same level as they started unless the dynamic changes.
10. Avoid wasted motion.

Always prepare the next motion IN ADVANCE.

VOLUME

Refer to "Volume" in Chapter 1

VOLUME EXERCISES

Play each line slowly. Form is more important than speed. Increase speed incrementally. Practice these exercises without sticks first. Use sticks when the form is correct. Use these repetitive exercises BEFORE introducing notation or as a supplement to reading music notation.

R = right hand high motion
L = left hand high motion
r = right hand low motion
l = left hand low motion

1. RRRR RRRR RRRR RRRR etc.
2. LLLL LLLL LLLL LLLL etc.
3. RRRR LLLL RRRR LLLL etc.
4. RRR LLL RRR LLL etc.
5. RR LL RR LL RR LL etc.
6. RLRLRLRLRLRLRLRL etc.

7. r r r r r r r r r r r r r r r r etc.
8. l l l l l l l l l l l l l l l l etc.
9. r r r r l l l l r r r r l l l l etc.
10. r r r l l l r r r l l l etc.
11. r r l l r r l l r r l l etc.
12. r l r l r l r l r l r l r l r l etc.

13. Rl l l Rl l l Rl l l Rl l l etc.
14. Lr r r Lr r r Lr r r Lr r r etc.
15. Rl l Rl l Rl l Rl l etc.
16. Lr r Lr r Lr r Lr r etc.

17. Rl Rl Rl Rl etc.
18. Lr Lr Lr Lr etc.
19. Rr Rr Rr Rr etc.
20. Ll Ll Ll Ll etc.
21. RLr l RLr l RLr l RLr l etc.

STICKING

The term "sticking" refers to the choice of right and/or left hand patterns that provide the most efficient method of achieving a desired musical result. A player's choice of sticking will determine how well a rhythmic passage is performed. The best sticking is determined by the desired musical effect.

Monitoring a percussionist's sticking at the early stages of development is very important. It is easy for a young student to develop habits that will cause permanent problems.

Keep in mind that:

- A percussionist must be able to perform equally well with both hands.
- Rhythmic patterns should be practiced with a variety of stickings.

Young players have a tendency to favor their strong hand. Avoid this tendency. If allowed to progress, they will start most rhythmic figures with the strong hand and start and end rolls with the strong hand. If this tendency is allowed to develop without giving equal attention to the weak hand, irreparable damage will result.

If young players hesitate while playing syncopated or rolled figures, it will most likely be attributed to **sticking.**

EXERCISE IN 3:1 RATIO TO STRENGTHEN WEAK HAND

The following exercise will aid in developing the weak hand. Practice this exercise at least twenty times daily. Play very slowly and loudly at first. Practicing on a pad is recommended. As the weak hand becomes stronger, increase the tempo and play at a variety of dynamic levels.

There are two generally recognized sticking systems: the **Alternating System** and the **Weak Hand System**. Many refer to the Weak Hand System as the "lead" system (or Right Hand Lead). For purposes of developing stronger players, the author chooses to apply the technique to the weak hand, thus enhancing overall playing ability. Each system has advantages and disadvantages in various musical settings.

1. ALTERNATING STICKING

The alternating system advocates a hand-to-hand approach to sticking. That is, if one begins playing with the left hand, then the right hand should follow and vice versa. There is a strict alternation of hands. This type of "sticking" helps young percussionists develop the ability to use each hand equally well. Alternating Sticking should be emphasized until the student is comfortable playing any figure with either hand.

Advantages of Alternating Sticking

1. Gives equal responsibility to both hands.
2. Can easily transfer to all other percussion instruments.
3. Recommended for fast passages.
4. Recommended for students who are partial to lead systems.

STICKING (cont.)

2. WEAK HAND STICKING

The weak hand system suggests that all primary pulses, principal beats, and strong accents be played with the "weak" hand and the remaining beats, up beats, and embellished notes be played with the other hand. Pick-ups with one or three notes start with the "strong" hand, two- or four-note pick-ups begin with the weak hand. Most rolls begin on the weak hand. The weak hand system is a structured system. If learned thoroughly, it may aid in sight-reading certain musical figures within a fairly narrow range of tempi.

Many refer to this sticking system as the "lead" system. For purposes of developing stronger players, the author chooses to apply the technique to the weak hand, thus enhancing overall playing ability.

EXAMPLES OF THE WEAK HAND STICKING SYSTEM

(assuming that the Left Hand is the weak hand)

1.

2.

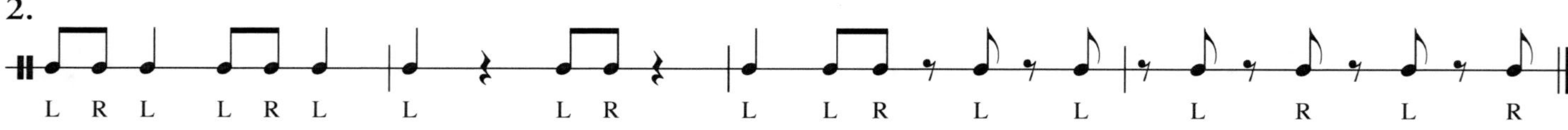

3.

4.

THE FLAM

Notation: ♪♩

The **flam** is an embellishment that adds duration and volume to a single note. A flam consists of a secondary note (notated as a grace note) played almost simultaneously with, but slightly before, a primary note.

Step-By-Step

1. Bending at the wrist (knuckles up), hold the right stick about 12 inches above the drum head and the left stick about one inch above the drum head. You are ready to play a right hand flam. Once the basic form of the flam is developed, the height of the highest stick will be determined by the dynamic.

2. Drop the sticks toward the instrument. The high stick will hit last.

3. Return to the original position. Do not allow the secondary note to raise beyond the original height (approximately one inch).

4. The primary note occurs in rhythm. In a practical sense, the secondary note has no time value.

5. Do not allow the sticks to move upward before the stroke motion begins. This results in wasted motion and will eventually cause the secondary note to become equal in height to the primary note.

Flams are either "closed" or "open." A closed flam refers to both sticks striking almost simultaneously, separated just enough to elongate the sound of a single note. "Open" refers to allowing more space to occur between the primary and secondary note. The amount of space is determined by the performer and the style of music. The performer must use his/her judgment as to which type of flam to use in each musical setting. Teachers should encourage percussionists to develop all variations of "open and "closed" flams.

STICKING (cont.)

FLAM SEQUENCE

Practice this sequence below, emphasizing good form, before attempting to play flams while reading music. Play each exercise slowly. As each pattern becomes comfortable, gradually increase speed incrementally. Flams are indicated by a uppercase R or L. The sequence will also work in developing ruffs (see page 41).

1. R R R R R R R R *etc.*
L L L L L L L L *etc.*

2. R l l l R l l l *etc.*
L r r r L r r r *etc.*

3. R l r l *etc.*
L r l r *etc.*

4. R l r L *etc.*
L r l R *etc.*

5. R r l *etc.*
L l r *etc.*

6. R r r *etc.*
L l l *etc.*

7. R l r L r l R l r L r l *etc.*

8. R r l l *etc.*
L l r r *etc.*

9. R r L l *etc.*
L l R r *etc.*

10. R l r r *etc.*
L r l l *etc.*

THE RUFF

Notation:

Ruffs are similar to flams except that they have two secondary notes rather than one.
Common stickings are illustrated below.

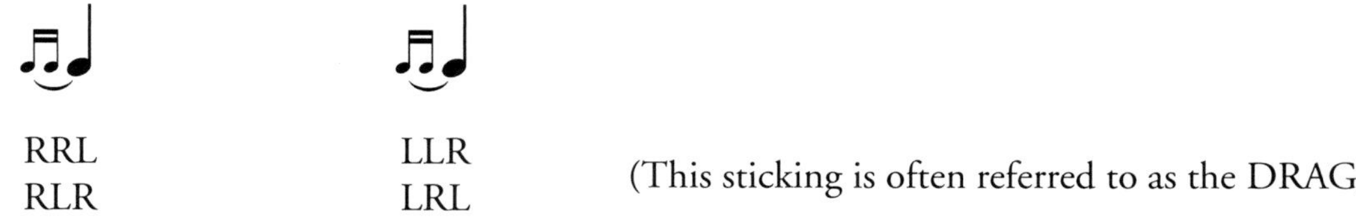

Ruffs, like flams, are played in open or closed style. The secondary notes in a "closed" ruff are often played as a "buzz" with one stick. This style is used most often in concert music. Use the Flam Sequence on page 35 to develop ruffs.

FOUR-NOTE RUFF

Notation:

The four-note ruff is similar to the three-note ruff except it has three secondary notes.

RLRL
LRLR

RRLR
LLRL

RLLR
LRRL

RRLL
LLRR

STICKING (cont.)

HOW TO DEVELOP THE FOUR-NOTE RUFF

Step-By-Step

1. Play the following patterns separately. Begin slowly and incrementally increase speed as the pattern becomes more comfortable to play.

2. Begin with both sticks held one dynamic higher than the desired dynamic level. For example, if the desired dynamic level is ***mf*** and the stick height representing ***mf*** is six inches above the instrument, hold the stick about nine inches above the head, the height for ***f***.

3. Drop the sticks toward the instrument allowing them to strike four independent times using the wrist and fingers. Think of making a single motion to achieve these four sounds. While it is recommended that one should think of making a single motion, there are actually four motions involved, but they happen within the context of one large, fluid motion. As this technique is developed, one can add emphasis to the first or last note of the four-note ruff. This is a fairly complex technique and will be difficult if the student has not acquired the prerequisite skills.

ROLLS

(Sustaining Sound)

Roll Notation:

The roll refers to a method of sustaining sound on percussion instruments. There are two types of rolls typically used on snare drum: the Concert Roll (also known as the buzz, multiple bounce, or closed roll) and the Open Roll (also known as the rudimental or double bounce roll). The Single Stroke Roll may also be used, but is less common on snare drum.

Beginning percussionists should learn the concert roll first, since it is usually easiest and applies to all types of playing. The open roll involves complex muscular coordination and has fewer applications in concert settings than the concert roll.

The roll should be introduced through rote exercises first. Introduce notation when students have a firm grasp of the basic technique. Correct form is imperative.

HOW TO DEVELOP A CONCERT ROLL

Step-By-Step

Method 1

1. The first prerequisite for learning the concert roll is for a student to understand and be able to play sixteenth notes (or the concept of four parts to one pulse).

2. Play the following pattern with alternating sticking. Students will normally be able to play this pattern at mf level. Let the student begin at the dynamic he/she feels most comfortable. The length of the pattern will vary among students. Some will need to have a shorter pattern involving sixteenth notes. Others will be able to play longer patterns.

3. Play the same pattern "buzzing" each sixteenth note.

4. Alter the patterns until a smooth, connected sound is achieved. This process takes time and patience.

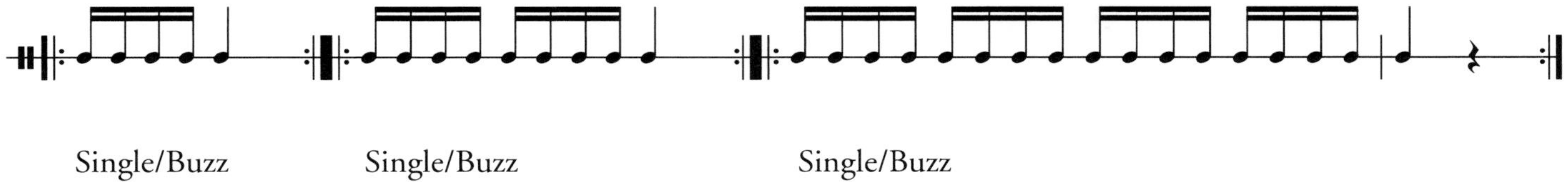

Single/Buzz Single/Buzz Single/Buzz

> The first prerequisite for learning a concert roll is for a student to understand and be able to play sixteenth notes (4:1 ratio).

NOTE: In order to achieve a "buzz," the fulcrum must be firm. Too much pressure will restrict the buzz; too little pressure will not produce enough buzz. Experiment with the pressure on the fulcrum until a full-sounding buzz is achieved with each stick.

Some students will be unable to immediately produce a sustained buzz with both hands. The weak hand will usually present problems. If this occurs introduce **Method 2**, but continue to practice **Method 1**.

ROLLS (cont.)

HOW TO DEVELOP A CONCERT ROLL (cont.)

Step-By-Step

Method 2

1. Play half notes at ♩ = 72 emphasizing a firm fulcrum. Allow each stick to buzz as many times as possible. Try to sustain the sound for the entire duration of a half note. Insist on a steady tempo.

2. Since it is likely that the weak hand will have more difficulty than the strong hand, practice the exercise using a ratio of three to one, with the weak hand playing three times as many motions as the strong hand.

S S   W W W W W W   S S   W W W W W W

S = strong hand   W = weak hand

3. Once both hands can play a sustained buzz, introduce quarter notes, then eighth notes, and so on. Alter the tempo as skill improves.

ROLL BASE
(Rhythmic Base)

Learning rolls by approaching each one with a specific roll base (rhythmic base) will ensure that percussionists will have complete control of rolls at all dynamics and tempi. Once a percussionist has complete control of the roll, he may find out that, under certain circumstances, a roll base is unnecessary. This will be true only of the mature percussionist.

All rolls should be based on a specific rhythm. The rhythm from which a roll is derived is called the roll base (rhythmic base). Most students will begin with a sixteenth note roll base. Adjustments may have to be made for others. Once a student can play connected, smooth rolls using a sixteenth note rhythmic base, they will be ready to experiment with other rhythmic values. Keep in mind that the student must understand the rhythmic base using single strokes first, then add the "buzz."

Two Variables that Affect Roll Base = TEMPO & VOLUME

TEMPO

A ***slow tempo*** requires ***more notes*** in the roll base. A ***fast tempo*** requires ***fewer notes.***

The examples on the next page illustrate how tempo determines roll base.

ROLL BASE (cont.)

VOLUME

A ***loud volume*** requires ***more notes*** in the roll base. A ***soft volume*** requires ***fewer notes*** in the roll base.

The examples below illustrate how volume determines roll base.

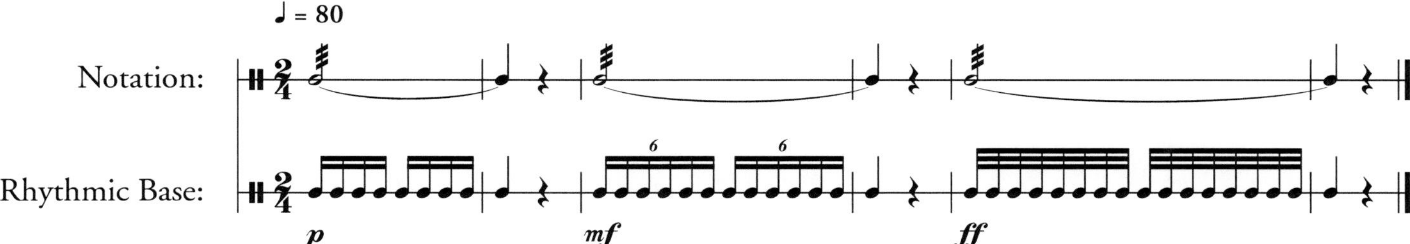

TIED ROLLS

Rolls will be written with or without ties. As a general rule, a roll that is tied will end on the note to which it is connected. A roll that is not tied will end slightly before the next rhythmic value. One or two notes of the rhythmic base are omitted on a non-tied roll.

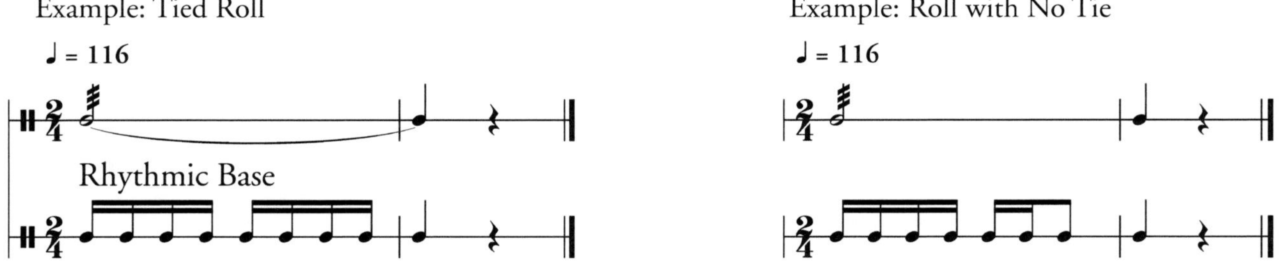

Roll notation, especially concerning ties, lacks consistency. Percussionists have to interpret roll notation since it is often inconsistent with the composer's aural intent. Musical sense takes precedence over musical notation. Use informed musical judgment and let the ear be the guide.

ROLLS (cont.)

OPEN ROLLS

As mentioned earlier, there are two types of rolls on the snare drum, the Concert Roll and Open Roll. Since the concert roll is used more often in concert settings and since it is much easier for young percussionists to learn, it should be mastered first. The open roll, however, should be introduced as soon as the student is able to play the concert roll with control at all dynamics and tempi.

The difference between performing buzz rolls and open rolls is in the firmness of the fulcrum. Buzz rolls require a firm fulcrum. Open rolls require a more relaxed fulcrum. Roll base is determined in the same manner for open as for closed rolls. The open roll involves two sounds per motion. For each wrist or arm motion, the stick is allowed to rebound once, resulting in two sounds per motion.

Open rolls are usually played within a fairly narrow tempo range (♩ = 92-120) using sixteenth notes as the roll base. However, they are adaptable to a wide range of tempi.

HOW TO INTRODUCE THE OPEN ROLL

Step-By-Step

1. Play a concert roll with a sixteenth note roll base. Keep a firm fulcrum.
2. While playing the concert roll with a sixteenth note rhythmic base, gradually relax the fulcrum.
3. You will find that at some point in relaxing the fulcrum, each motion of the wrist or arm will produce two sounds instead of a buzz. When this is achieved, you are playing the open roll.
4. Experiment with the amount of pressure on the fulcrum to determine how much is needed to produce an open roll.

EXAMPLES OF OPEN ROLLS

(Five-Stroke, Seven-Stroke, Nine-Stroke, and Thirteen-Stroke)

One will see snare drum solos and method books that refer to rolls by the number of "hits" (strokes), such as five-stroke, seven-stroke, and nine-stroke rolls. These are open rolls. Examples of these rudimental rolls are given below.

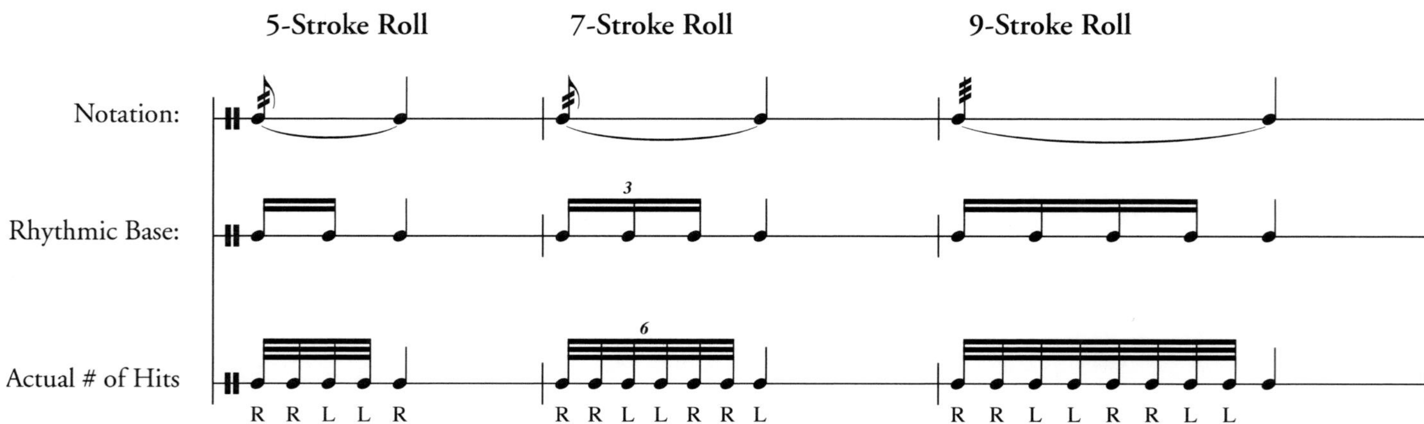

Avoid the tendency to teach rolls by referring to the number of strokes or hits per roll. Always refer to the rhythmic value of the roll, or roll base.

INTRODUCTORY ROLL EXERCISES

Exercises should be practiced starting rolls with either hand.

RUDIMENTS

Rudiments are a limited number of rhythmic figures that reflect a very small percentage of what a snare drummer needs to know. While practicing these rhythmic patterns for long periods will help develop "chops", developing snare drum technique on such a limited perspective may have a negative effect on one's overall musical development.

Snare drum method books that are based on a rudimental approach, snare drum solos, class method books, and other sources related to percussion pedagogy frequently refer to the "Standard Drum Rudiments" or the "International PAS Rudiments." Until recently, the study of snare drum centered around rudiments as a primary means of developing technique. However, it is important for the percussion pedagogue to understand the historical significance of rudiments so that their use in educational settings can be viewed in perspective.

Rudiments have their origin in military drumming. In earlier times, military commanders would communicate with the troops through a series of rhythmic signals played on drums. Select rhythmic patterns were also used to announce various functions during a soldier's day and served an important role in ceremonial events. Since most drummers during this time did not read music, and since the rhythmic patterns were not notated, they were learned by rote and passed on generation after generation. Eventually the patterns were notated and referred to by names, what we call rudiments today. Snare drum solos often used in school settings today are based on a series of rhythmic figures called rudiments.

Many of the snare drum books available today reflect the same format for learning snare drum as the first books for military drumming in the 1700s and 1800s. For lack of another systematic method of learning snare drum that is available to music educators on a mass scale, rudiments are still taught today. While it is not as common today as it once was, many states require rudiments as a part of the audition for honor groups.

Since the exclusive practice of the standard rudiments may inhibit the ultimate musicianship of a snare drummer, a more enlightened approach to learning snare drum is recommended. For example, percussionists should extract patterns from their music and practice with as many stickings and dynamic variations as possible. Rhythmic patterns used to develop technique should come directly from band and orchestra parts, good solos, and percussion ensemble parts. In other words, develop percussionists' overall musicianship rather than memorizing a limited number of figures with predetermined stickings that may or may not apply to specific musical settings.

Imagine, for a moment, that the following two-measure phrase is an excerpt from a typical composition for band or orchestra, percussion ensemble, or solo snare drum. A percussionist may experience difficulty playing any part or the entire excerpt. Any difficulty a student may encounter (circled figures indicate potential problem spots) can be "fixed" through the following procedure. (Refer to "How to Use Patterns to Develop Technical/Musical Skill" on page 49.)

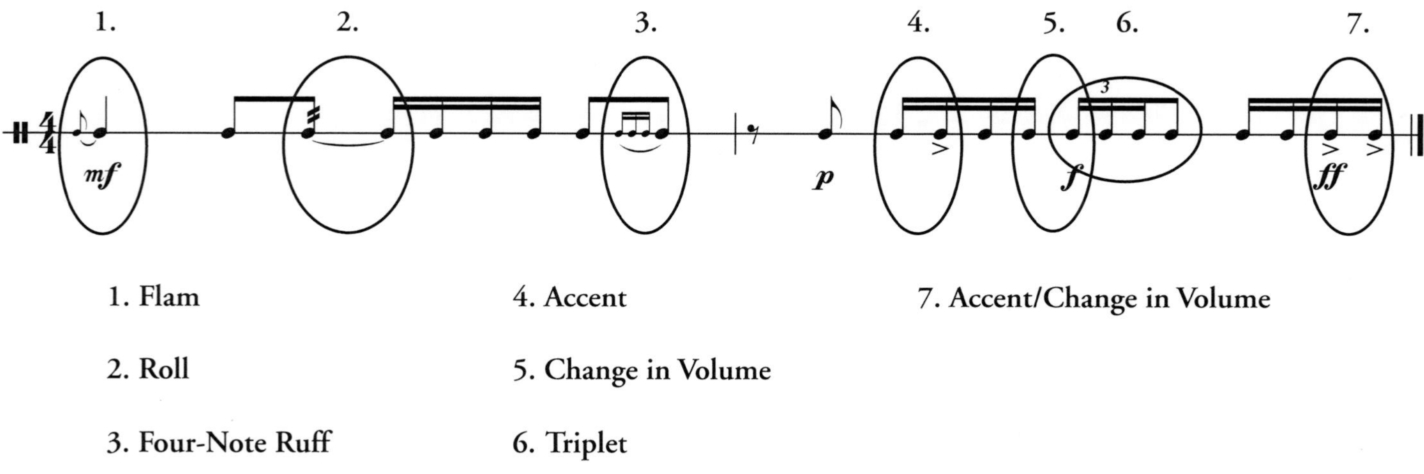

HOW TO USE PATTERNS TO DEVELOP TECHNICAL/MUSICAL SKILL
(Extracting Patterns from Music)

Step-By-Step

1. Identify the technical problem (such as stick height, roll development, etc.) for every figure.
2. Isolate the figure and play it very slowly at the correct dynamic. It must be played perfectly at a very slow tempo.
3. Once the figure can be played at a very slow tempo, increase the speed by ten to fifteen beats per minute. Play the figure at this tempo until the performer is consistent.
4. Continue incremental increases in tempo until the desired tempo is achieved.
5. Once the performer is able to play one figure correctly, go to the next one.
6. Begin connecting figures. For example, play the first and second figure as a separate exercise.
7. Do not practice figures by starting slowly, increasing speed and returning to the original tempo. Always maintain a consistent tempo.

Rhythmic figures extracted from one's performance library form the basis of a percussionist's technical/musical exercises and etudes. They serve specific needs directly related to the music one encounters.

STICK SELECTION

Step-By-Step

1. The stick should be straight.
2. Each pair must be of equal weight.
3. Stick size:
    - Avoid sticks that are very large or too small in diameter. They are difficult to control.
    - It is better to have a slightly larger stick than one that is too small.
4. Drum size:
    - A large drum will require a larger stick while a small drum will require a smaller stick.
5. Types of bead:
    - There are three types: oval, round, and slightly tapered with no apparent bead.
    - The bead may be made of nylon or the same material as the shaft. Nylon-tipped sticks are not recommended for concert or marching percussion.
    - A round bead usually allows for more control and works best on snare drum (concert and marching).
    - The oval bead is used mostly on drum set and cymbals because more surface area is exposed and is in contact with the cymbal, hence producing more sound. However, this is the type of bead found most often in full service music stores.
    - Wood tips are best and should be used for all general playing.
    - Nylon tips should only be used for drum set since they are able to produce a brighter tone on the cymbal allowing it to cut through the band. It is not essential that nylon tipped sticks be used for drum set playing, especially if the cymbal is of superior quality. Nylon tips break and come off easily.

STICK SELECTION (cont.)

6. Type of material (Sticks are made of a variety of woods and aluminum):
   - Maple wood is very durable
   - Oak is durable
   - Hickory is less reliable. Use caution when purchasing.
7. Style of music:
   - Marching, concert band, drum set, orchestra, marches, waltzes, ballads, etc.
   - Style of music and type of drum used will largely determine the type of stick used.

Classification systems are not standardized among manufacturers. A logical approach to this confusing market is to become familiar with one or two of the more widely used models and use them as a point of reference. For example, manufactured sticks are classified by one of three letters (A, B, S) preceded by a number. The number designates the size and shape of the bead and shaft. The larger the number, the smaller the stick and vice versa.

1. A Series: small, lightweight
2. B Series: general purpose, medium size
3. S Series: large marching stick

PARTS OF THE SNARE DRUM

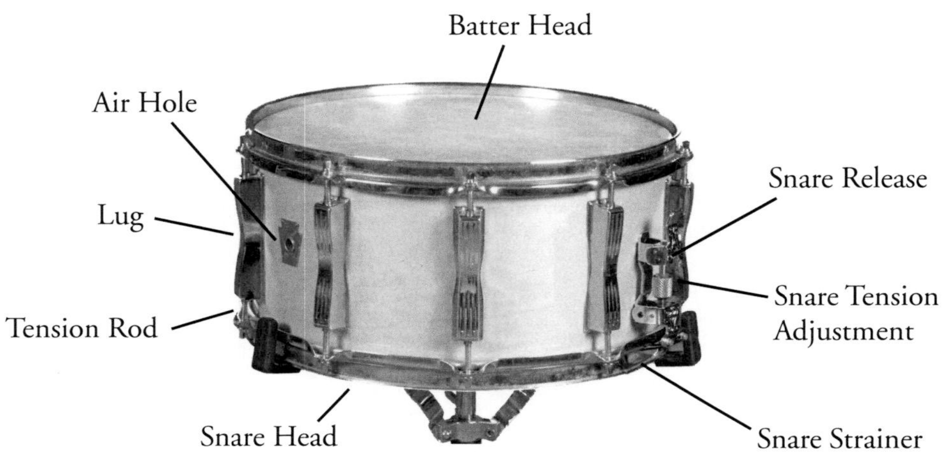

SIZES OF SNARE DRUMS

There are a variety of sizes of snare drums, each fulfilling specific musical needs. The most common sizes follow:

1. 3-1/2 x 13" Piccolo (rarely used): Concert Band, Orchestra, Percussion Ensemble
2. 5-1/2 x 14": Concert Band, Orchestra, Percussion Ensemble, Drum Set (most common size)
3. 6-1/2 x 14": Concert Band, Orchestra, Percussion Ensemble, Drum Set
4. 12 x 15" (14"): Marching, Military Music in Concert Band or Orchestra

Snare drum shells are available in a variety of materials:

1. Wood Shell – dark sound
2. Metal Shell (bronze, aluminum, brass, etc.) – brighter sound than wood
3. Fiberglass – durable, similar to wood sound

PREVENTIVE MAINTENANCE

The snare drum requires very little maintenance beyond changing heads and adjusting snares. Observe the following precautions in order to avoid unnecessary damage.

1. Always store the instrument in a safe place away from objects that might fall on it.
2. Keep the head clean.
3. Do not allow the drum stand to touch the bottom head. This will puncture the head.
4. Always check the snare drum stand, making sure that it does not fall.
5. Never allow anyone except a percussionist to play the instrument.
6. Do not leave the instrument set up in an area where others might knock it over.
7. Never write on the drum head.
8. Never store near a heat source.
9. Never over-tighten heads.
10. Never place objects on the head.

SELECTING A DRUM HEAD

There are two heads on a snare drum: the batter head (top) and the snare head (bottom). Drum heads must be replaced occasionally to ensure the best possible sound. The primary considerations for head selection should be the musical situation (concert band, marching, jazz) and the desired sound. It is not necessary to wait until a head breaks to replace it. The head may have lost its musical effectiveness long before then. A drum head should be replaced under the following conditions:

1. When the head loses its resilience.
2. When the top of the counterhoop is even with the shell.
3. When the head has been punctured.
4. When the head is excessively dirty and cannot be cleaned.
5. When the head has a slow stick response.
6. When there is a loss of tonal resonance.

The thickness of a drum head is measured in mils. One mil is one-thousandth of an inch. Generally, use a head of medium thickness (7 mil) for the batter head on a concert snare drum and a thicker head (10 to 15 mil) for the batter heads of marching percussion. A snare head, or the bottom head on a snare drum, is thinner (usually 2 to 3 mil).

Batter heads are available in a variety of types:

Clear:	Not suitable for brush work
White (smooth):	Not suitable for brush work
White (coated):	Recommended
Fiberskyn:	Recommended. Close to the texture of calfskin.
Kevlar:	Specifically designed for marching drums. Very durable. Not suitable for concert snare drum playing.

MOUNTING A DRUM HEAD

Step-By-Step

1. Loosen the tension rods until they can be pulled out of the lugs.
2. Remove the counterhoop and head to be replaced or cleaned.
3. Wipe off dust and dirt accumulated around edge of shell.
4. Fit new head over shell.
5. Remount and align counterhoop.
6. Replace tension rods and screw them down by hand until snug.
7. Using a drum key, give each rod one full turn. Tune opposite, not adjacent rods (see example below).
8. Test for sound with drum stick. Apply more tension if needed.
9. Final tuning of the batter head should result in a head that can be depressed only slightly by pressing thumb down in the center of the head.

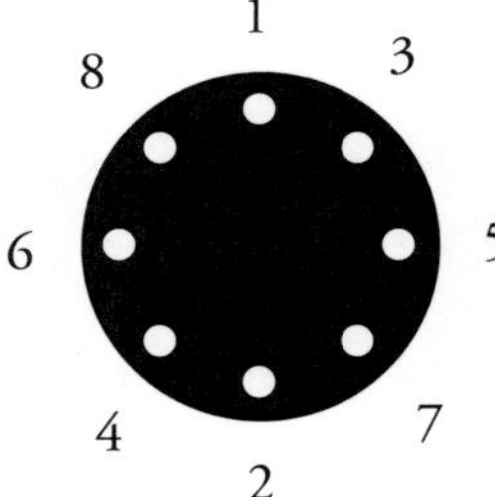

NOTE: When replacing and tuning the snare head, it will be necessary to remove the snares. Follow the same mounting procedure as the batter head.

TYPES OF SNARES

A snare is anything that is stretched across the bottom head of the drum that vibrates when the batter head is struck and results in a "buzzing" sound. There are several types of snares.

1. **Wire** – Very metallic sound, durable, unaffected by changes in climate. Recommended for school use.
2. **Gut** – Dark sound, affected by changes in climate unless treated. Expensive. Not recommended for schools.
3. **Nylon Covered Cable** – Very durable, similar to gut. Not available for all drums. Recommended, if available.

INTERNAL MUFFLER/EXTERNAL MUFFLER

Many snare drums are equipped with an internal muffler that can be adjusted to fit against the bottom of the batter head with varying degrees of pressure. The internal muffler should rarely be used since it changes the quality of sound by restricting the vibrating pattern of the drum.

Most snare drums will have a certain amount of "ring." This is actually desirable in typical concert settings. A small amount of "ring" helps project the sound. Young percussionists, however, often try to eliminate all of the ring, thinking that it is an undesirable quality.

An external muffler is any soft object (such as a handkerchief) placed on the drum head to achieve a "dry" sound. It is commonly used to decrease the sound of the instrument or to reduce head vibration in order to achieve the sound required by the composer. Avoid the tendency to tape external mufflers to a drum head. This is another tendency of young percussionists in an effort to imitate recorded sounds.

SITTING *vs.* STANDING

Once a student has acquired good playing habits, it is acceptable to sit while playing the snare drum. Good posture is essential. Both feet should be flat on the floor and the upper part of the body should be erect. Proper drum height should be observed. If percussionists are allowed to sit, an adjustable stool should be obtained. One will rarely see professional percussionists sitting while playing snare drum since they often have to play several instruments in close succession, and sitting would restrict movement.

PRACTICE PAD *vs.* SNARE DRUM

When practicing the snare drum, a percussionist has three option in terms of the choice of instrument: a snare drum, practice pad, or another type of pad that fits on top of the snare drum. A beginning percussionist has several purchase options:

- A drum kit with snare drum and snare drum stand.
- A drum kit with snare drum, stand, and rubber pad for the drum.
- A drum kit with practice pad and bells.
- A drum kit with snare drum, bells, and rubber pad for the drum.

Most practicing should be on a snare drum. However, for technical exercises that must be played loud and for long periods, a pad is recommended. A pad that is mounted on a stand with adjustable height is recommended. Avoid pads that have to be laid on a tabletop. It is unlikely that they will be able to be played at the correct height and with the correct posture.

Some school systems furnish snare drums for the students. If this occurs, it is important that each student has either a pad or a drum at home for practicing.

Pads are excellent for developing dexterity and facility. They are recommended for certain kinds of practice, but they do not feel like a real drum.

SELECT SNARE DRUM RESOURCES

Snare drum literature is constantly changing. Feel free to edit this brief list as needed.

SNARE DRUM SOLOS

Six Unaccompanied Solos for Snare Drum	M. Colgrass	Law-Gould
Style Suite	M. Houllif	C. Alan Publications, LLC
Three Dances	W. Benson	Warner/Chappell Music

SNARE DRUM METHOD BOOKS/COLLECTIONS

Book of Percussion Audition Music, The	N. Daughtrey/C. McClaren	C. Alan Publications, LLC
Performing Percussionist, The	J. Coffin	C.L. Barnhouse, Inc.
Sequential Approach to Fundamental SD, A	Tom Morgan	C. Alan Publications, LLC

SNARE DRUM STUDIES

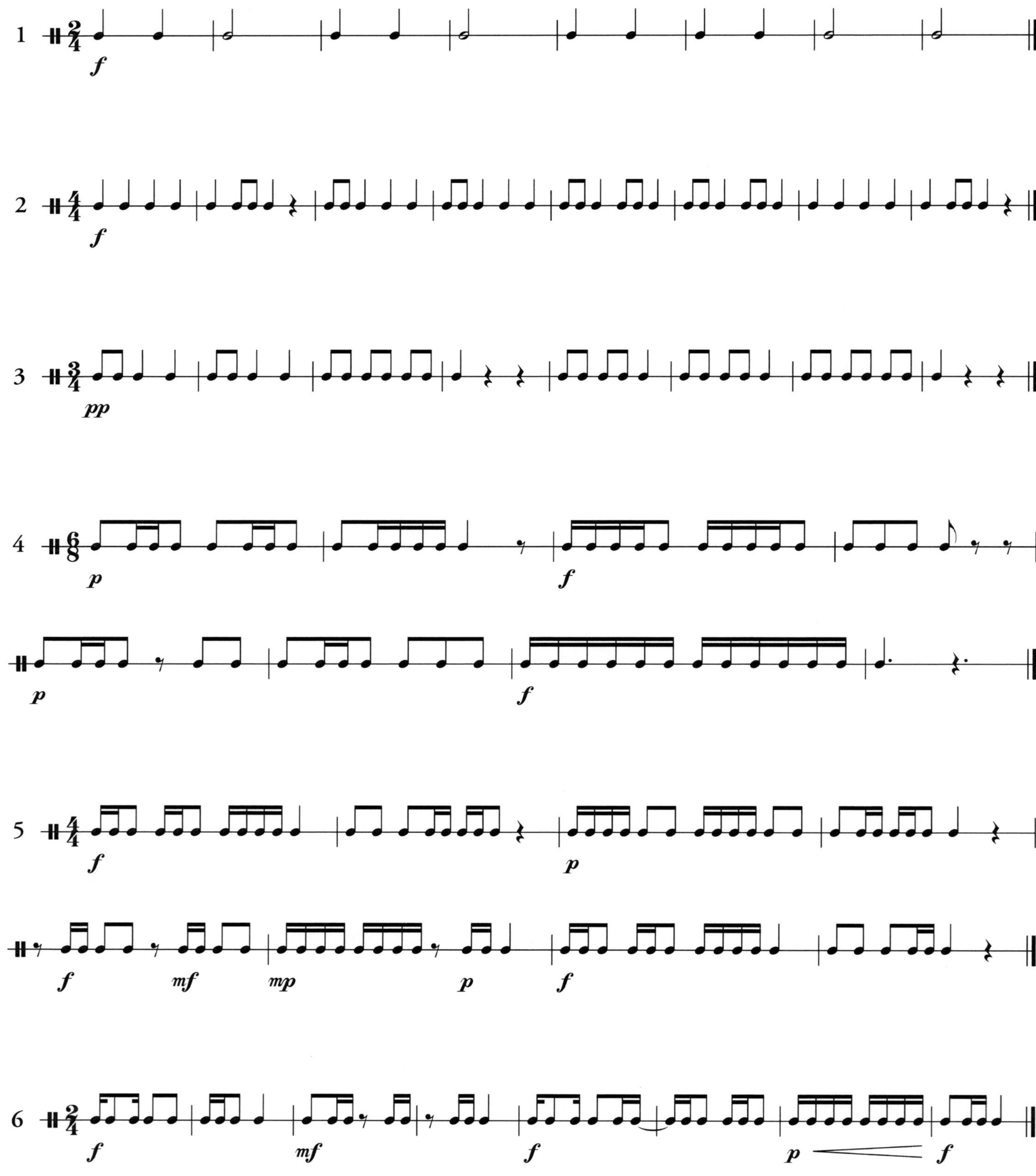

Dynamic Control

Flams

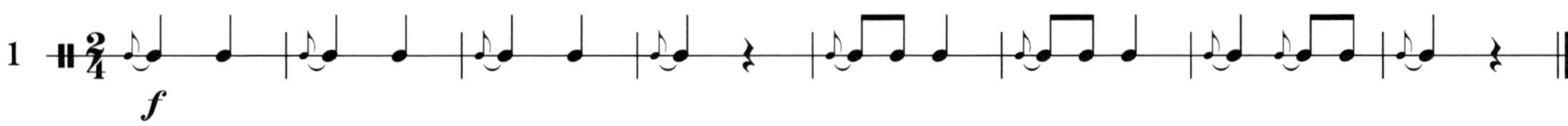

Ruffs

Rolls

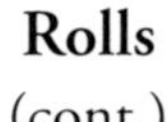

Rolls
(cont.)

Etude No. 1

Etude No. 2

Etude No. 3

Write an etude that might serve as a final exam for a graduating senior in high school.

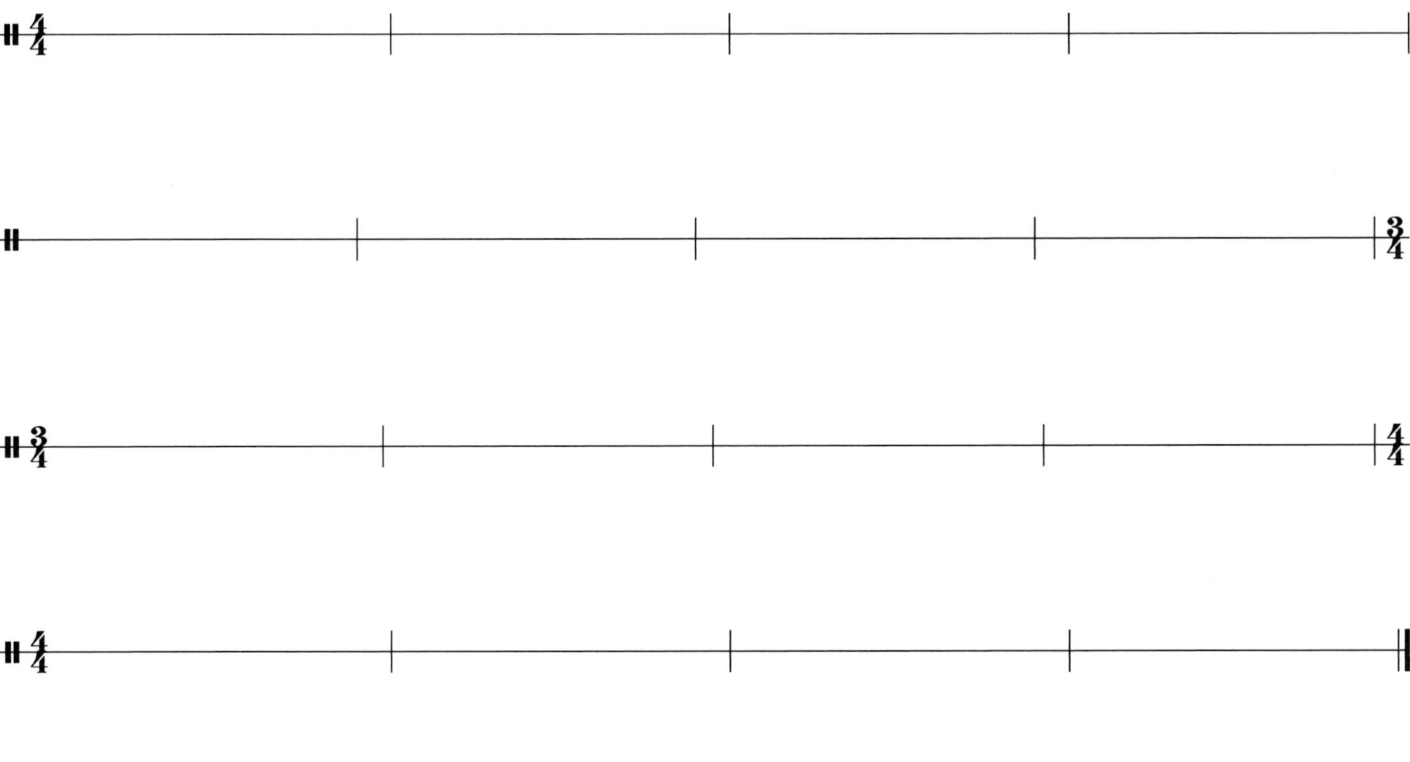

Chapter 4

TIMPANI

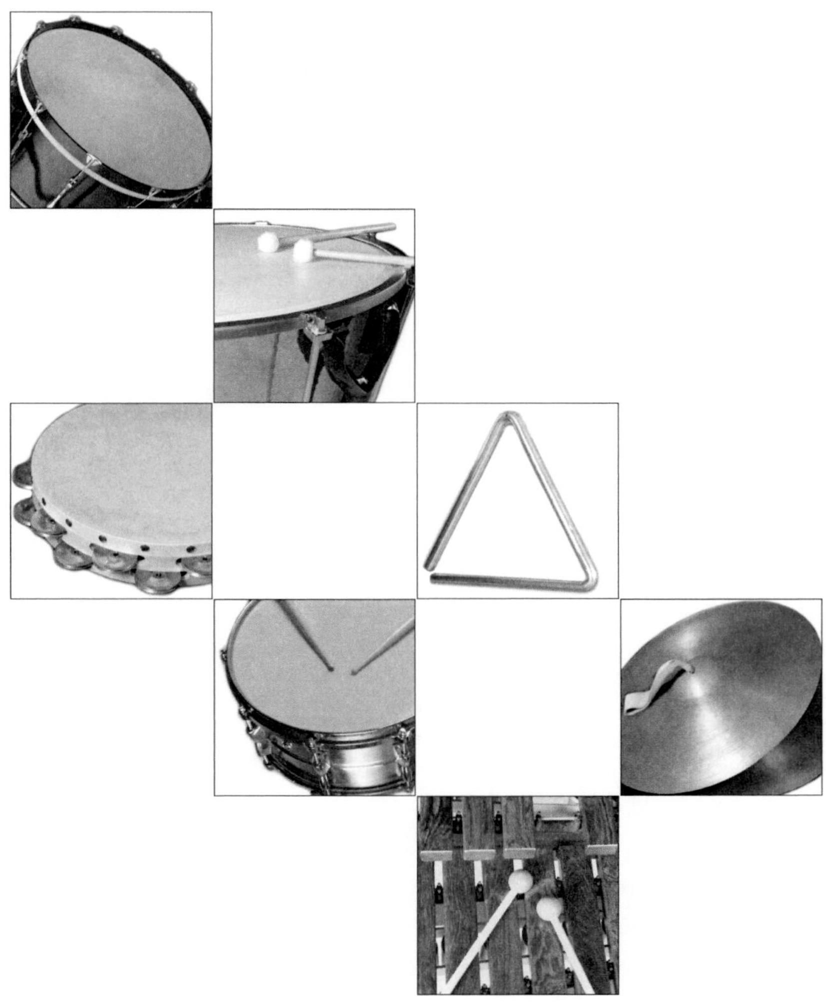

Chapter 4

TIMPANI

The Common Elements

Posture
Grip
Striking Motion
Volume
Sticking
Rolls

THE IMPORTANCE OF TIMPANI

In the scheme of percussion performance, timpani ranks as one of the most important instruments. Along with snare drum and keyboard percussion, timpani will be at the center of percussionists' playing experience. It is a prestigious position in most large ensembles. The teacher's attitude is the key to establishing good playing habits in young percussionists. Teaching timpani simply requires knowing the fundamental issues involved in timpani performance and developing activities that help young people acquire specific skills.

WHEN AND HOW TO START PLAYING TIMPANI

A young percussionist can learn certain timpani skills before actually playing the instrument. That is, there are a number of timpani skills that one can develop while playing the snare drum, keyboard percussion, and other percussion instruments. One of the most important aspects of early timpani training is acquiring the ability to match pitch with one's voice by singing scales, arpeggios, etc. Require percussionists to sing with the band while they warm up or play a composition. With practice, they can do this while playing snare drum, bells, or other percussion instruments.

A percussionist is usually ready to begin playing timpani when the following criteria have been met.

- The student demonstrates adequate snare drum technique. While this is helpful, it is not essential.
- The student can internalize pitch (match pitch, sing desired pitches). Internalizing pitch is often difficult for percussionists with little or no experience in singing. The physical skills involved in playing timpani will progress more rapidly in individuals with more experience in pitch discrimination (ear training). If teachers fail to incorporate pitch discrimination in timpani instruction, students will always be deficient in this area. Ear training should begin long before formally introducing timpani.
- The student is tall enough to play the instrument correctly.

Timpani should be formally introduced to percussionists. Set aside a time after or during the regularly scheduled band rehearsal to introduce the basics of timpani performance. This can be accomplished in fifteen to thirty minutes. Or, take five minutes and introduce one or two items at a time. Do not leave anything to chance. After an item is introduced, it must be closely monitored until firmly established.

MINIMUM TIMPANI SKILLS FOR HIGH SCHOOL GRADUATES

	Student Names			
1. Demonstrate good posture and fluid movement while playing.				
2. Play on correct playing area of the instrument.				
3. Demonstrate correct grip.				
4. Demonstrate piston motion.				
5. Demonstrate use of stick height to attain desired dynamic level.				
6. Demonstrate a working knowledge of multiple-line sticking.				
7. Perform rolls at all dynamic levels and in all ranges using appropriate roll speed.				
8. Read bass clef fluently.				
9. Tune any pitch on the appropriate drum using the 5-step tuning method.				
10. Know sizes and approximate ranges of each timpani.				
11. Demonstrate muffling technique				
12. Select appropriate mallets for a variety of musical situations.				
13. Demonstrate proper care and maintenance of the instrument.				

THE 30-MINUTE INTRODUCTION

Some teachers prefer to introduce basic timpani skills to all percussionists at once. A logical sequence for introducing timpani in a thirty-minute session is listed below. This list of timpani techniques serves only as an introduction to timpani. Other items need to be introduced as the need arises. Each of these items are discussed in detail later in this chapter.

Step-By-Step

1. Describe the Grip
2. Playing Area
3. Where to Stand (Posture)
4. Striking Motion
5. Tuning
6. Muffling
7. Rolls
8. Mallet Selection
9. Bass Clef
10. Size and Range of Each Timpani
11. Sticking will take more time and most likely will be a part of the ongoing process of learning to play timpani. However, the rules for multiple-line sticking must be outlined and formally introduced to all percussionists.

Items 9 and 10 may require more time, depending on students' previous knowledge of pitch reading.

SIZE AND RANGE

In the United States, timpani are usually arranged with the largest timpani on the performer's left, progressing to the smallest on the performer's right. The range of each instrument corresponds to its size: the largest diameter has the lowest pitch range and smallest diameter has the highest pitch range.

Although there are several sizes of timpani, the most common sizes and the ***fundamental pitch*** for each is provided below. The approximate range of each drum is a fifth. The fundamental pitch is usually the lowest practical pitch on an instrument.

Set-Up from Left to Right

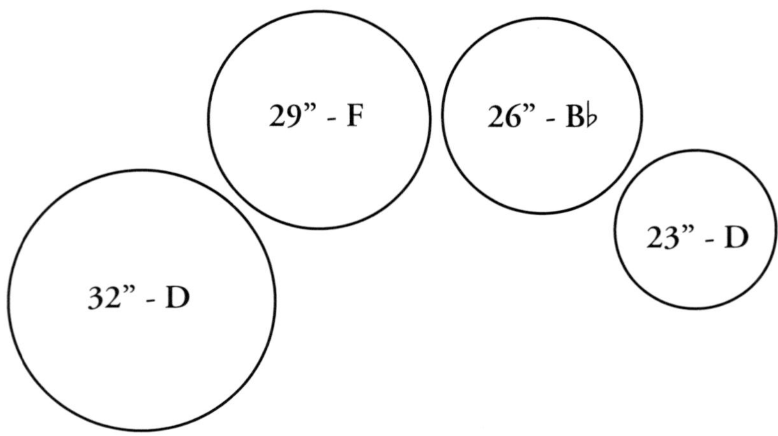

Timpani should be set up with the lowest drum to the left and the highest drum to the right.

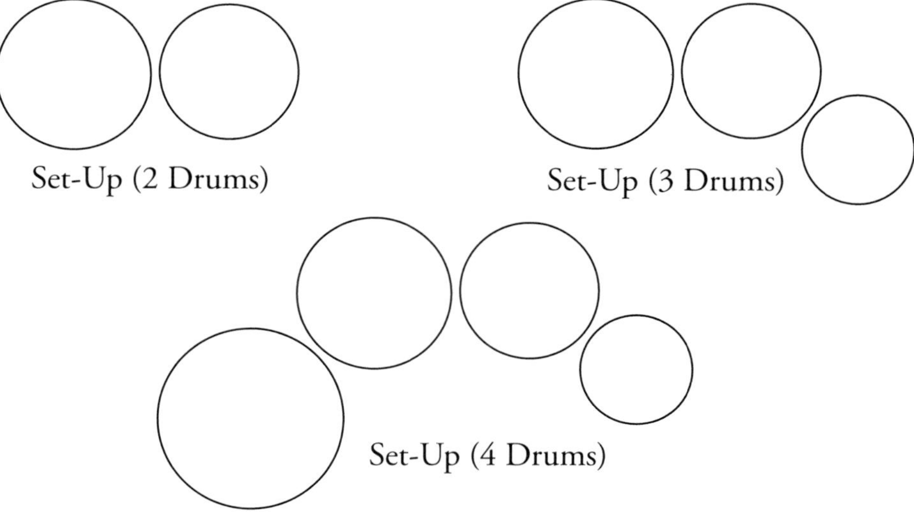

POSTURE

Like snare drum, there are four factors that determine good posture on timpani:

1. Baseline
2. Height
3. Playing Area
4. Distance of Body from the Timpani

BASELINE

Baseline refers to the relaxed, natural position of the body. Determine the baseline position by simply walking in a free, unencumbered manner, as if going for an evening stroll in the park. Always establish the body's natural baseline posture before playing an instrument. Keep the head up.

HEIGHT

Unlike snare drum, timpani are usually not height adjustable. Young percussionists will need to stand while playing timpani since they are usually not tall enough to sit and maintain correct posture. However, once the player acquires adequate technique and is able to tune confidently, he/she may sit while playing. In fact, it is almost essential to sit when playing music that requires frequent tuning changes. While sitting,

1. Apply the rules of correct posture.

2. Sit on a swivel stool with adjustable height.

3. The feet should always be on the floor or on the timpani pedals.

POSTURE (cont.)

PLAYING AREA

Consider four points when determining the correct playing area on timpani.

1. Desired Sound
2. Distance from the Edge of the Drum Head
3. Playing Area Relative to the Entire Head
4. Body Position

The procedure below requires students to determine the correct playing area by listening for the best sound. Students determine for themselves where one needs to strike in order to produce the best sound.

HOW TO DETERMINE THE CORRECT PLAYING AREA

Step-By-Step

1. Ask the student to tap the timpani head (***mf***) starting at the extreme edge.

2. Continue to tap the head while gradually moving toward the center of the head. Ask the student to listen to the different sounds produced.

3. Continue to tap the head and gradually move back toward the edge.

4. Repeat the process several times asking the student to describe the changes in sound that occur while moving the mallet from the edge to the center and back.

5. Finally, ask the student to stop on the spot that has the most resonant (ringing) sound. This will be the best playing area. Repeat this process on each drum.

Distance from the edge is one thing to consider when determining the correct playing area. Another consideration is the placement of two mallets on the timpani head and their relationship to the entire head. The picture below illustrates this point. Mallets should not be too close to one another. Each mallet should have its own playing spot at equal distances from the edge.

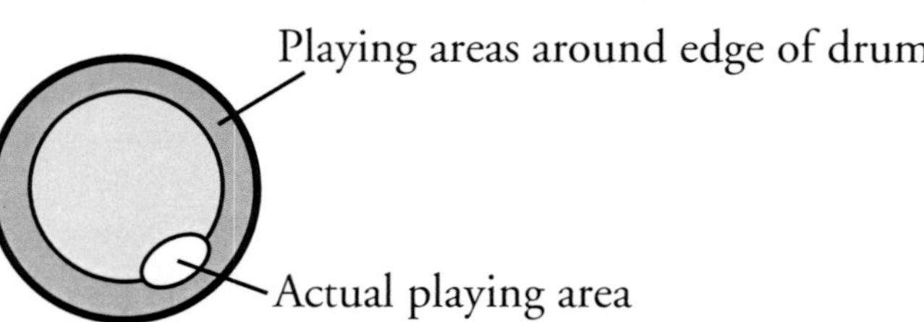

DISTANCE OF BODY FROM THE DRUM

The timpanist should be a comfortable distance from the instrument that allows the body to maneuver freely. Follow the procedure below for determining the correct distance from the instrument.

Step-By-Step

1. Holding a mallet in each hand (see Grip discussion on next page), stand several feet away from the instrument.
2. Hold the mallets in the proper playing position, as if ready to play with one on each of the two inside timpani (29" and 26").
3. Step toward the instrument so that each mallet is in the correct playing area on the two inside timpani. While moving toward the instrument, be sure to keep the upper arm in-line with the body. Do not allow the arms to move forward or backward.
4. When the mallets are in the correct playing area, you have reached the correct distance from the drum.
5. Without moving the arms forward or backward, and while keeping the feet in place, turn to the right until the mallets are on the highest two drums. (Note: If the right mallet is not on the correct playing area on the highest drum, do not adjust the body. Adjust the drum so that when the process in this step is repeated, the mallet will automatically fall in the correct spot.)
6. Repeat Step 5, moving to the left and adjusting the lowest drum to accommodate the body.

When the drums are adjusted to "fit" the body's relaxed posture, the player should have easy access to all four timpani by simply turning the upper body and leaving the feet in place.

GRIP

The matched grip (refer to the chapter on Snare Drum for an explanation) will transfer from snare drum to timpani. Unless a student shows extreme interest and is willing to seek private instruction, the matched grip will be adequate throughout high school. If a student's achievement is beyond the norm and indicates a desire to enter the music profession, it may be advisable to introduce the French Grip (thumbs-up grip). However, most percussionists are able to learn the French Grip upon entering college if they have acquired good basic skills during middle school and high school.

INTRODUCTION TO THE FRENCH GRIP

Step-By-Step

Without Mallets

1. Without mallets, assume the correct position for matched grip with palms down.
2. Rotate hands so that palms face each other with thumbs up. Form a "C" with each hand.
3. Keeping the forearms parallel to the floor, move hands together until thumbs and fingertips touch.
4. Rotate hands back and forth in a smooth circular motion, so that the thumbs point alternating toward and away from the body.
5. While continuing this back-and-forth circular movement, separate hands 1 to 2 inches. Be sure that the movement in each hand remains the same as before, so that the hands are mirror images of one another. Refer to Steps 3 and 4 as often as necessary to ensure proper hand position.

GRIP (cont.)

Step-By-Step

With Mallets

1. With mallets, assume the correct position for matched grip with palms down.
2. Without changing anything, rotate hands so that palms face each other, thumbs up.
3. Using the same back-and-forth circular movement as in Step 4 above, move mallets in a straight line, perpendicular to the drum head.

French Grip
(overhead view)

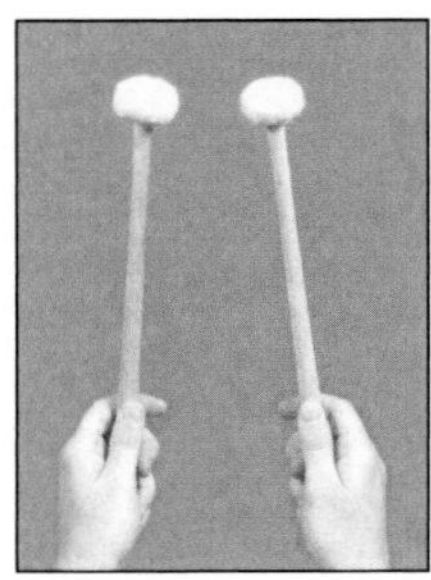

STRIKING MOTION & VOLUME

The striking motion (Piston Motion) and volume for timpani is identical to that described in Chapter 1.

STICKING

Follow the guidelines under MULTIPLE-LINE STICKING in Chapter 1.

CROSS-STICKING

Occasionally, there will be a need to cross-stick while playing timpani. In general, one should avoid cross-sticking, but sometimes it is unavoidable.

When cross-sticking, always cross the wrists. This will ensure that the mallets will strike in the correct playing area. In the example above, where the right hand crosses over the left, the right wrist should be on top of the left wrist when the cross-sticking occurs (indicated by an "X").

Cross Sticking
(overhead view)

Left Hand Right Hand

ROLLS

(Sustaining Sound)

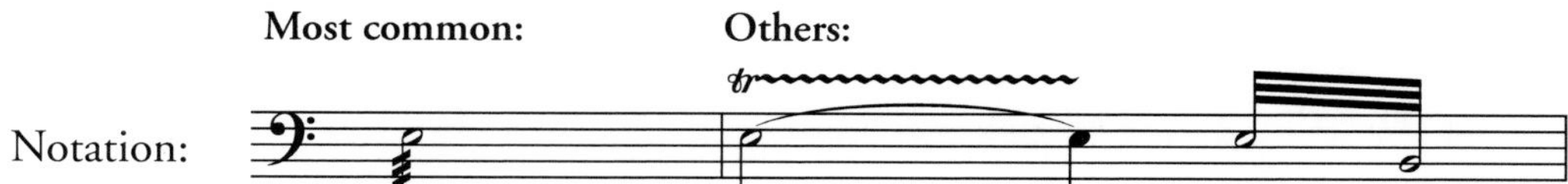

A timpani roll is produced by playing single notes, one after another, creating a sustained sound. In general, rolls should be played as slow as possible while still achieving a sustained sound. Two main factors determine roll speed: **PITCH** and **VOLUME.**

Pitch

A drum head vibrates slower on a low pitch and faster on a higher pitch. Likewise, a slow vibration requires a slower moving single stroke while a fast vibrating head will require the stick to move faster in order to maintain a sustained sound.

Lower Pitch = Slower Roll Speed **Higher Pitch = Faster Roll Speed**

Volume

Like a snare drum roll, a soft dynamic requires fewer hits than a loud volume

Softer Volume = Slower Roll Speed **Louder Volume = Faster Roll Speed**

The mallets' impact must be in phase with the rate of vibration of the timpani head. If the roll becomes out of phase with the vibration of the head, a "popping" or "choked" tone or void spots in the tone will result. This is caused by the mallet colliding with the upward or downward vibration of the head, rather than being perfectly in sync with it.

A **forte-piano roll** (***fp***) is common in timpani playing. Follow the procedure below to produce the **forte-piano roll** effect.

Step-By-Step

1. Strike the drum with a single mallet.
2. Allow the vibrations to die away until the sound reaches the degree of softness desired.
3. Resume the roll without making stick noise.

TUNING

Well-tuned timpani may make the difference between an average and an outstanding performance. Likewise, percussionists who properly tune timpani make the difference between an average and an exemplary music program.

While most band and orchestra directors agree that properly tuned timpani are important to the overall intonation of an ensemble, a clearly defined method for teaching tuning remains a mysterious phenomenon. The simple, five-step tuning method of timpani tuning presented here will take the mystery out of tuning and place the process in a more practical perspective.

There are two types of timpani tuning. The first occurs when a head must be replaced or removed from the bowl for cleaning. It involves adjusting all tuning rods until the pitch at each rod is identical. This process is called "tempering" and simply means that a timpani is in tune with itself.

The second type of tuning assumes that a timpani head is "tempered." It is the most common type and involves tuning (usually with the aid of a pedal) to specific pitches that occur in various compositions. While both types of tuning are important, the latter is used most often by young percussionists and should be of primary concern to directors and students. The following five-step process requires minimum knowledge from directors and students. However, when developed, it will solve most timpani tuning problems.

FIVE-STEP TUNING METHOD

Step-By-Step

1. **Obtain the Lowest Pitch**
   The timpani head should be in its most relaxed position. On balanced-action timpani, the heel of the foot is near the floor while the toe points up.

2. **Listen to the Pitch**
   Listen to the desired pitch using a fixed source such as a pitch pipe, piano, or any other instrument with relatively stable pitch.

3. **Sing the Pitch**
   This is one of the most important steps in the process as it relates to a percussionist's total development. Pitch must be internalized if one expects any musician to play in tune (singers, brass and woodwind players, and percussionists). Take time for this important step. Great vocal production is not essential, but unless students internalize pitch, their ability to tune without the aid of a director will always be underdeveloped.

4. **Strike the Timpani ONCE**
   Strike the timpani once and quickly move the pedal until the desired pitch is obtained. One often observes timpanists striking a drum several times while moving the pedal up and down, searching for the pitch. Subsequently, he/she forgets the correct pitch and turns to the director for help. To avoid this, strike the drum once and move the pedal quickly before the pitch is forgotten or the head stops vibrating.

5. **Stop on the Desired Pitch**
   This step is actually the conclusion of Step 4. During the early stages of learning to tune timpani, however, it is not unusual to over-shoot the desired pitch. If this happens, return to Step 1. Do not adjust the pitch downward, but rather begin the process again. The timpani is more likely to hold the pitch by moving the pedal "up" instead of "down" into the pitch.

KEYS TO SUCCESSFUL TIMPANI TUNING

Remember, timpani tuning is a complex skill that takes time and practice to develop. One should devote as much time to developing percussionists' musicianship as we devote to developing the musical skills of wind and string players. Develop a rotating schedule that requires all percussionists to play (and tune) timpani during warm-up with the full ensemble as well as other times during the rehearsal.

Timpani heads must be in good condition. The world's finest timpanist cannot tune heads that are either damaged or not tempered (See page 71).

During the initial stages of learning to tune, percussionists may feel unsure about singing. If this occurs, ask the entire ensemble to sing the desired pitch along with the timpanist and the percussion section. This will make percussionists feel more at ease while raising the level of awareness of other musicians.

Start singing at the beginning level. Every time other instrumentalists play a scale, long tone, or arpeggio, require all percussionists to sing. Then, when the need to learn how to tune timpani occurs, it is more likely that pitch will be internalized and singing in front of other musicians will be perfectly normal.

TUNING GAUGES

Tuning gauges are mechanisms that attach to each individual timpani and indicate the approximate pitch. There are several types and models of tuning gauges: some attach to the pedal and some are connected to the timpani bowl. **The best tuning gauge is the timpanist's ear.** In general, young percussionists should avoid using tuning gauges. Young percussionists need to develop their ability to hear and match pitches. Using tuning gauges often prevents one from determining for him/herself whether a pitch is accurate. In addition, gauges need constant adjustment and must be carefully monitored. If gauges are not checked daily, a timpanist will receive inaccurate readings, resulting in further damage to his/her sense of pitch.

CHANGING PITCHES WHILE PLAYING (Pedaling)

It is often necessary to change pitches in the middle of a piece of music. The composer usually allots adequate time for such pitch changes. Follow the procedure given below for changing pitches. The tempo will determine how much time can be allowed for each step in the process. A rhythmic approach where each step occurs on a specific beat may be helpful.

Step-By-Step

1. Quietly strike the drum to determine its current pitch.
2. Sing the desired pitch.
3. Tune the drum to the desired pitch from the current pitch.
4. Check the accuracy of the desired pitch.

In order for a player to change pitches in this manner, he/she must have the ability to:

- Focus on his/her pitch while "tuning out" the other players in the group.
- Know and be able to sing intervals from any given pitch.
- Use intervallic relationships to determine the desired pitch based on the current pitch
- Keep good time while accomplishing the pitch change(s).

MUFFLING

Muffling is the process of stopping the vibration of the timpani head by placing a hand (or parts thereof) on the head. Since a timpani head vibrates long enough to create a sustained sound, the vibration must be stopped occasionally. Muffling is achieved by pressing the fingertips plus the base of the hand on the head, depending on the dynamic. **A loud sound will require the fingertips plus the base of the hand, while a softer dynamic will require only the fingertips.**

A timpani head can be muffled with the hand that is used to strike the instrument or the opposite hand, depending on which is most appropriate at the time. When the entire hand is used to muffle, the shaft of the mallet is at a right angle to the hand. In a sense, one must change the grip slightly in order to muffle.

The precise timing of muffling is important in order to produce the exact note value intended by the composer. In the example below, in order to give the half note its full value, one should muffle on beat three of measure 1 and beat four in measure 2. Occasionally the note values written by the composer or arranger are meaningless, so the player must determine muffling by using good musical sense. There are occasions when one will let a note ring longer than notated. Also, in some passages, there simply is not sufficient time to muffle, whatever the note values may be.

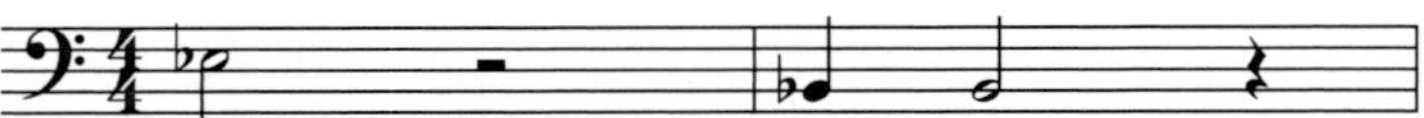

Occasionally, although only one timpani is struck, both or all of the drums must be muffled. This is to prevent the drum which is not struck from ringing "sympathetically." When using more than two drums, a general rule to follow is to muffle the last two drums struck (first), then move immediately to the other drums.

There may be an occasion when a timpanist is required to muffle one drum while simultaneously playing another drum. This permits only one sound to occur at a time. See the example below.

MALLET SELECTION

A wide variety of timpani mallets are available. The style of music should determine the type of mallet used in any given situation. In general, the articulation of a timpani mallet is determined by the type and weight of the core and the type of felt used:

Hard core and thin felt → **Articulate**
Softer core and thick felt → **Less Articulate**

A core of medium hardness with medium-thick felt (such as "Staccato" mallets) will provide enough articulation for most playing situations. Avoid playing with mallets that are extremely soft. They do not provide the most characteristic timpani tone.

PARTS OF THE TIMPANI

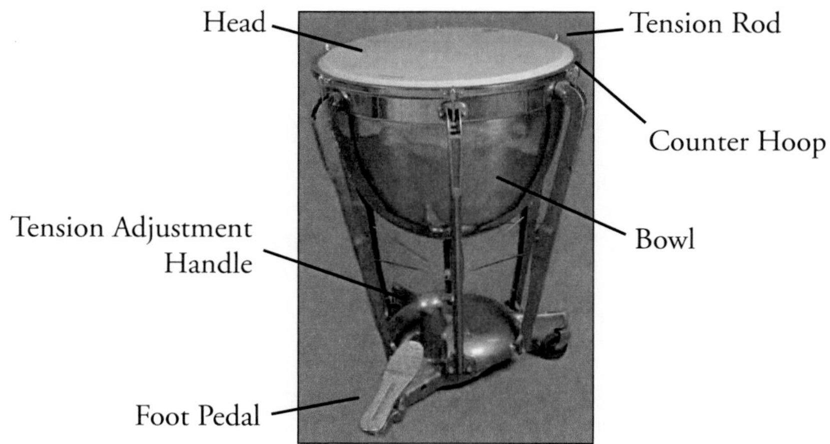

REPLACING AND FINE-TUNING A TIMPANI HEAD

One of the most critical aspects of playing timpani is the ability to mount and fine-tune a timpani head so that it "sings" with a true tone. A head that is not in tune with itself (tempered) and cannot hold a true pitch will be the cause of many intonation problems for any band or orchestra. Follow the procedure below for mounting and fine-tuning a timpani head.

Step-By-Step

1. Unscrew all lug screws and remove the counterhoop and old head. If you are going to put the old head back on the bowl, mark it so that it can be replaced in exactly the same position. Once a plastic head is seated, it does not respond well to constant tampering.

2. Clean and lubricate all moving parts.

3. Clean the lip of the bowl.

4. Rub a small amount of lubricant (Hydrous lanolin, silicone spray) with your fingers on the lip of the bowl. Too little causes squeaks and too much makes the tone dull.

5. If you are reusing the old head, clean it and place it on the bowl. If you are replacing the old head with a new one, place it on the bowl.

6. Place counterhoop over the head.

7. Center the head and counterhoop.

8. Set the tension screws. Using the fingers, apply enough tension to eliminate the wrinkles in the head. Use the "opposites" system (refer to snare drum page 52).

9. Turn all screws back once to see where the head wrinkles first.

10. Apply more tension to that area.

REPLACING AND FINE-TUNING A TIMPANI HEAD (cont.)

11. Turn all the tension screws so that they face the same way. Work in quarter turns and half turns. Avoid large turns that will throw the head out of balance.

12. Making sure to turn all screws that same amount, tighten the head to the fundamental pitch.

13. If each step has been carefully observed, the head should be centered. If not, begin again.

14. Play a mezzo-forte (***mf***) note and listen to the general pitch of the head.

15. With two fingers resting in the center of the head, tap softly at each point of tension (pole). Match the pitch of each tension point to the general pitch of the head.

16. If one pole is out of tune, check its opposite before making any change.

17. Then, adjust the one that is out of tune. You may have to repeat this process many times. Always re-check the general pitch of the head. This fine-tuning takes practice and patience. Never work for more than a few minutes on fine-tuning so that you don't lose concentration and confuse pitches.

A new drum head will stretch and change pitch after a certain amount of playing. The new head will need to be fine-tuned daily for a week or more and once a week thereafter.

SELECT TIMPANI RESOURCES

TIMPANI SOLOS

Airs	Y. Goto	C. Alan Publications, LLC
Ballad for the Dance	S. Goodman	CPP/Belwin
Sonata for Timpani	J. Beck	Boston Music
Toccata for Timpani	E.L. Dimer	C. Alan Publications, LLC

TIMPANI METHOD BOOKS/COLLECTIONS

The Book of Percussion Audition Music	N. Daughtrey/C. McClaren	C. Alan Publications, LLC
The Complete Timpani Method	A. Friese/A. Lepak	Warner Bros. Publications
Five Pieces for Timpani	J. Metzger	C. Alan Publications, LLC
Modern Method for Tympani	S. Goodman	Warner Bros. Publications

TIMPANI STUDIES

Basic Technique

Muffling

Rolls

Cross-Sticking

Multiple-Line Sticking
(Time & Distance)

Four Timpani

Tuning

Pedaling

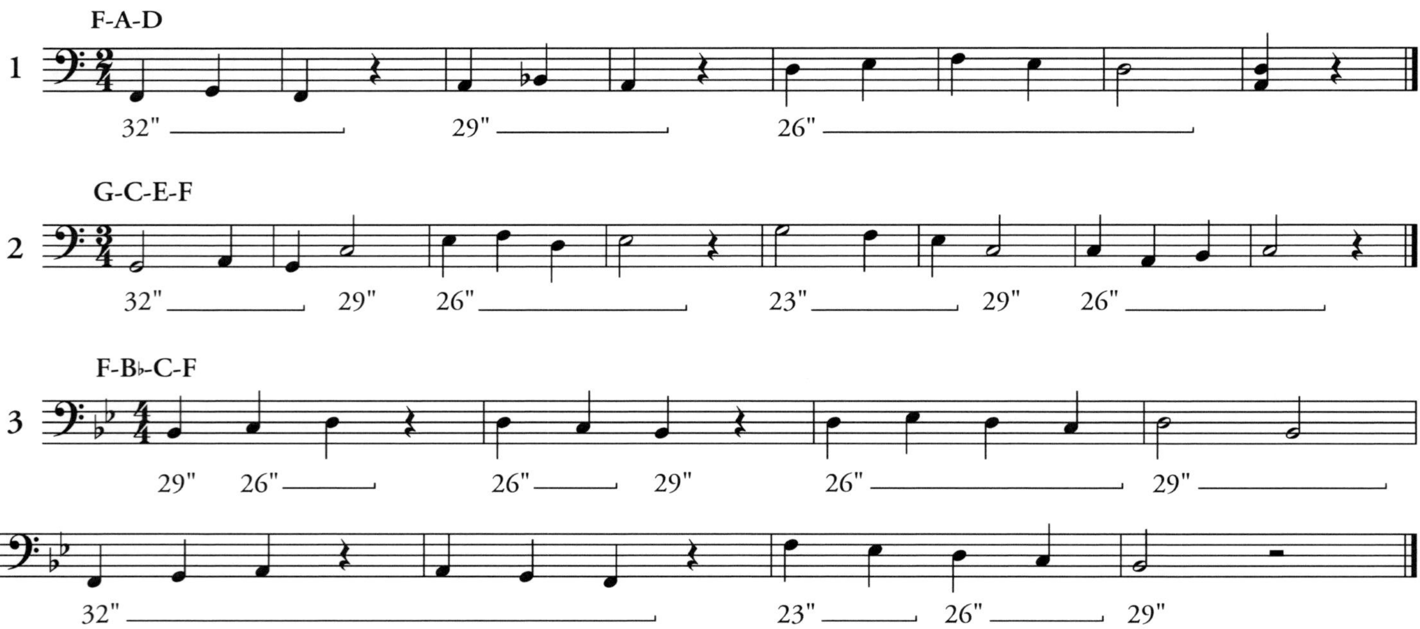

Chapter 5

KEYBOARD PERCUSSION

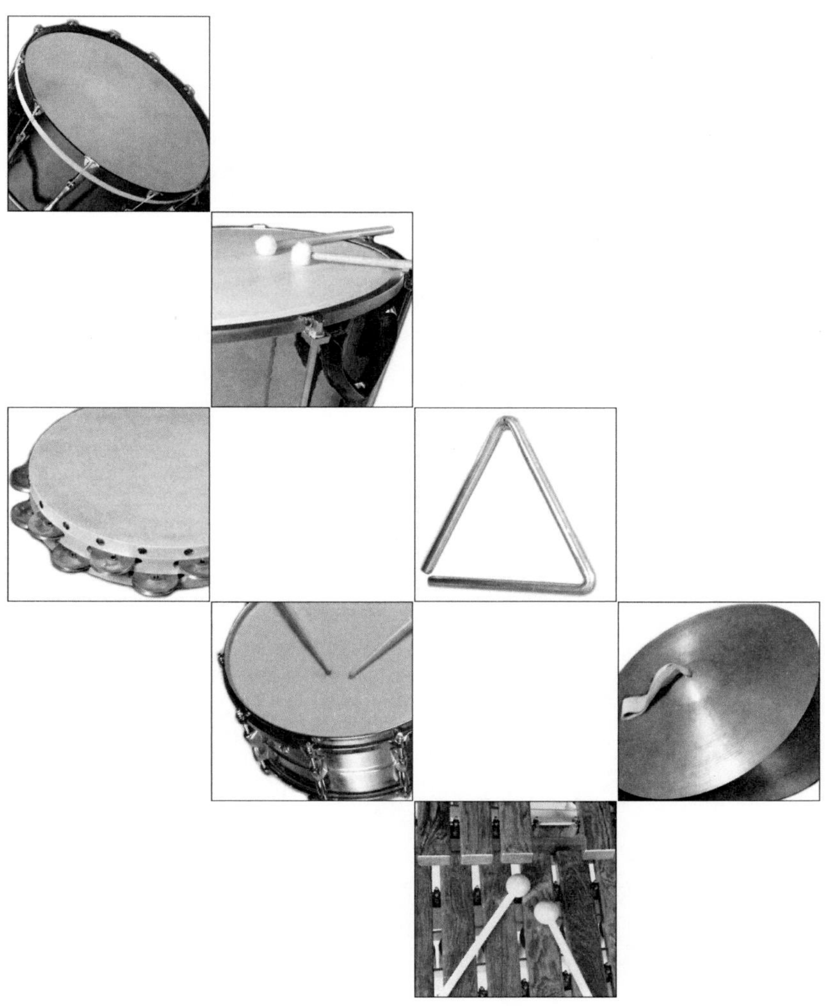

Chapter 5

KEYBOARD PERCUSSION

The Common Elements

Posture
Grip
Striking Motion
Volume
Sticking
Rolls

In realistic performance situations, percussionists are expected to perform competently on all basic percussion instruments including keyboard percussion instruments (marimba, xylophone, bells, chimes, and vibraphone). Keyboard percussion performance skills are crucial to the development of young percussionist's musical and technical abilities.

The teacher's attitude toward keyboard percussion and its importance in the beginning stages of development is the key to establishing good playing habits in young percussionists.

If keyboard percussion skills are not started and monitored from the onset of instruction, it is less likely that they will ever develop to their fullest potential.

MINIMUM KEYBOARD PERCUSSION SKILLS FOR HIGH SCHOOL GRADUATES

	Student Names			
1. Demonstrate good posture and fluid movement while playing.				
2. Play on correct playing area of the instrument.				
3. Demonstrate correct two- and four-mallet grips.				
4. Demonstrate piston motion using two and four mallets, including four-mallet stroke types.				
5. Demonstrate use of stick height to attain desired dynamic level.				
6. Demonstrate a working knowledge of how to determine appropriate sticking.				
7. Demonstrate two- and four-mallet rolls at all dynamic levels throughout the instrument range using appropriate roll speed.				
8. Read treble and bass clef fluently.				
9. Play scales and demonstrate a working knowledge of key signatures.				
10. Demonstrate a working knowledge of the differences (physical and technical) between bells, vibraphone, chimes, marimba, and xylophone.				
11. Demonstrate basic dampening and pedaling techniques on vibraphone.				
12. Select appropriate mallets for a variety of musical situations.				
13. Demonstrate proper care and maintenance of the instruments.				

POSTURE

Posture in keyboard percussion performance, in part, is dependent on the height of the instrument. The height of many keyboard percussion instruments is not easily adjusted because the instruments are constructed at a fixed height. Therefore, the ideal instrument height as achieved in playing snare drum may not be possible. Some manufacturers of keyboard percussion instruments have designed instruments with height adjustment devices. However, these instruments may not be designed for frequent height changes.

If an instrument is too low, it may be placed on small wooden blocks for additional height. If an instrument is too tall, it may be lowered by removing the wheels. Otherwise, little can be done except perhaps building a platform the length of the instrument on which the percussionist may stand while playing. Such a platform would need to be carefully constructed and should extend well under the instrument and far enough behind the percussionist to provide ease of movement with no danger of falling off. This is not recommended.

PLAYING AREA

On most keyboard percussion instruments, excluding chimes, there are several possible playing areas.

1. Directly in the center of the bar
2. Slightly off center
3. On the extreme edge of the bar (accidental bars only)
4. The node, or the point of least vibration (where the string runs through the bar).

The general purpose playing areas are **slightly off center** and **on the extreme edge** (accidentals only). Each area produces a slightly different tone. Areas 2 and 3 are probably the closest in tone color. The **node** (area 4) is the least resonant part of the bar and produces a dull tone. Therefore, playing on the node should be avoided. Mature percussionists sometimes use the node as a playing area to achieve special effects, such as subtle decrescendos. However, beginners should avoid playing on the nodes.

One should listen continually for consistent tone quality from bar to bar via consistent playing area.

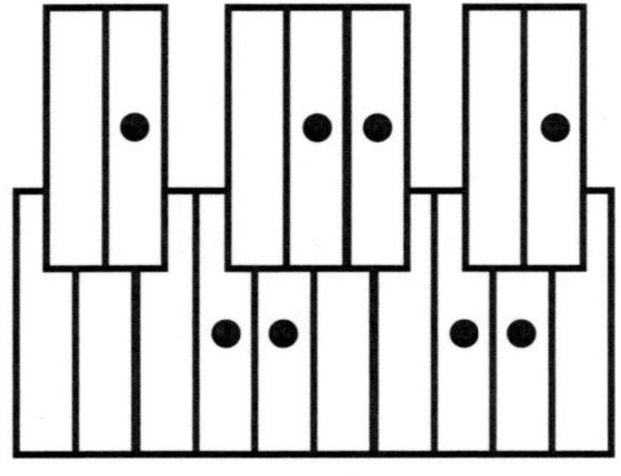

E♭ Major Scale: All Center
(CORRECT)

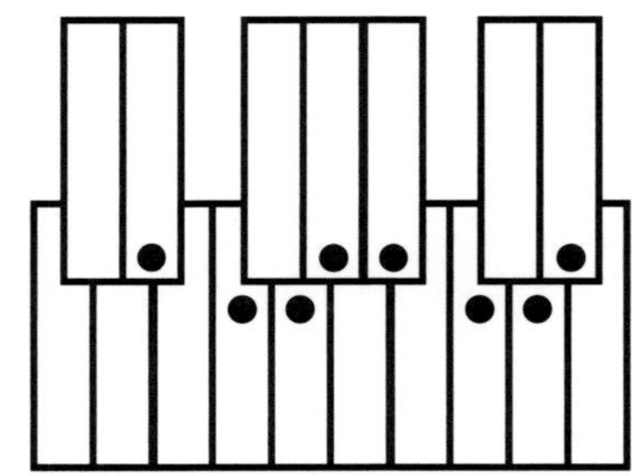

E♭ Major Scale: Off Center & Edge
(CORRECT)

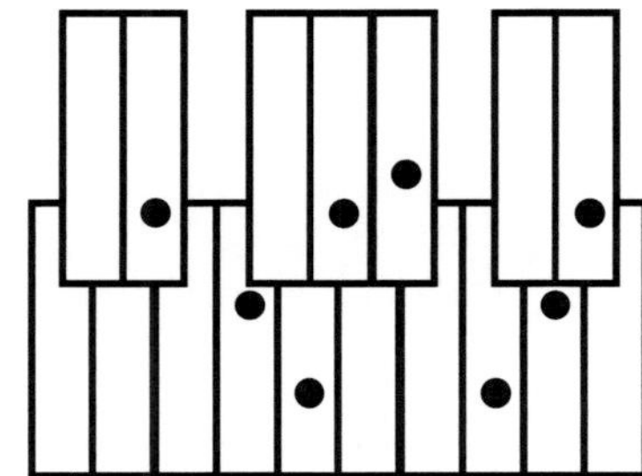

E♭ Major Scale: Off Center & Node
(INCORRECT)

The student should be given opportunities to experience the differences in tone quality attributed to playing area through guided experimentation. Experiment with playing area and make choices as to where bars should be struck for best tone.

For example:

1. On the pitch "F," begin striking the bar repeatedly at the extreme edge and continue striking as you move to the center of the bar. Then move back out to the extreme edge. Discuss the differences in tone.

2. Teach the first five pitches of the "F" scale by rote. Have the student:

    - Play up and down the five-note scale in the center of the bar.
    - Play just off center of the bar.
    - Play the B-flat within the scale on the extreme edge of the bar.
    - Play the B-flat within the scale on the node.

    Discuss the differences in tone throughout the exploration. (Bell kits are more limited in playing area because of bar size. This exercise is better suited for a full-sized instrument.)

Tempo and ***melodic patterns*** influence playing area. Keep in mind that "natural" and "accidental" corresponds to white and black keys on a piano keyboard.

1. If the tempo is slow to moderate and the melodic pattern does not contain awkward sticking combinations, one should play in the center or slightly off center on both natural and accidental bars.

2. If the tempo is fast or the melodic pattern contains awkward sticking combinations, play the "accidental" pitches on the extreme edge of the bar and the natural pitches slightly off center to increase movement efficiency.

POSTURE (cont.)

TRACKING

Tracking is a term that refers to allowing one mallet to rest slightly ahead or behind the other (Fig. 3-1). The purpose of tracking is to avoid the feeling that one mallet is going to get in the way of the other by positioning one mallet in one playing area over the bar and the other mallet in another playing area over the bar (Fig. 3-2). When both mallets play "natural" bars, the mallets usually rest off center, on each side of the resonator (Fig. 3-3). When both mallets play "accidental" bars, the mallets may rest off center or with one mallet in the center and one at the edge of the bar (Fig. 3-4). Orchestra bells and vibraphone should be struck in the center of the bar whenever possible.

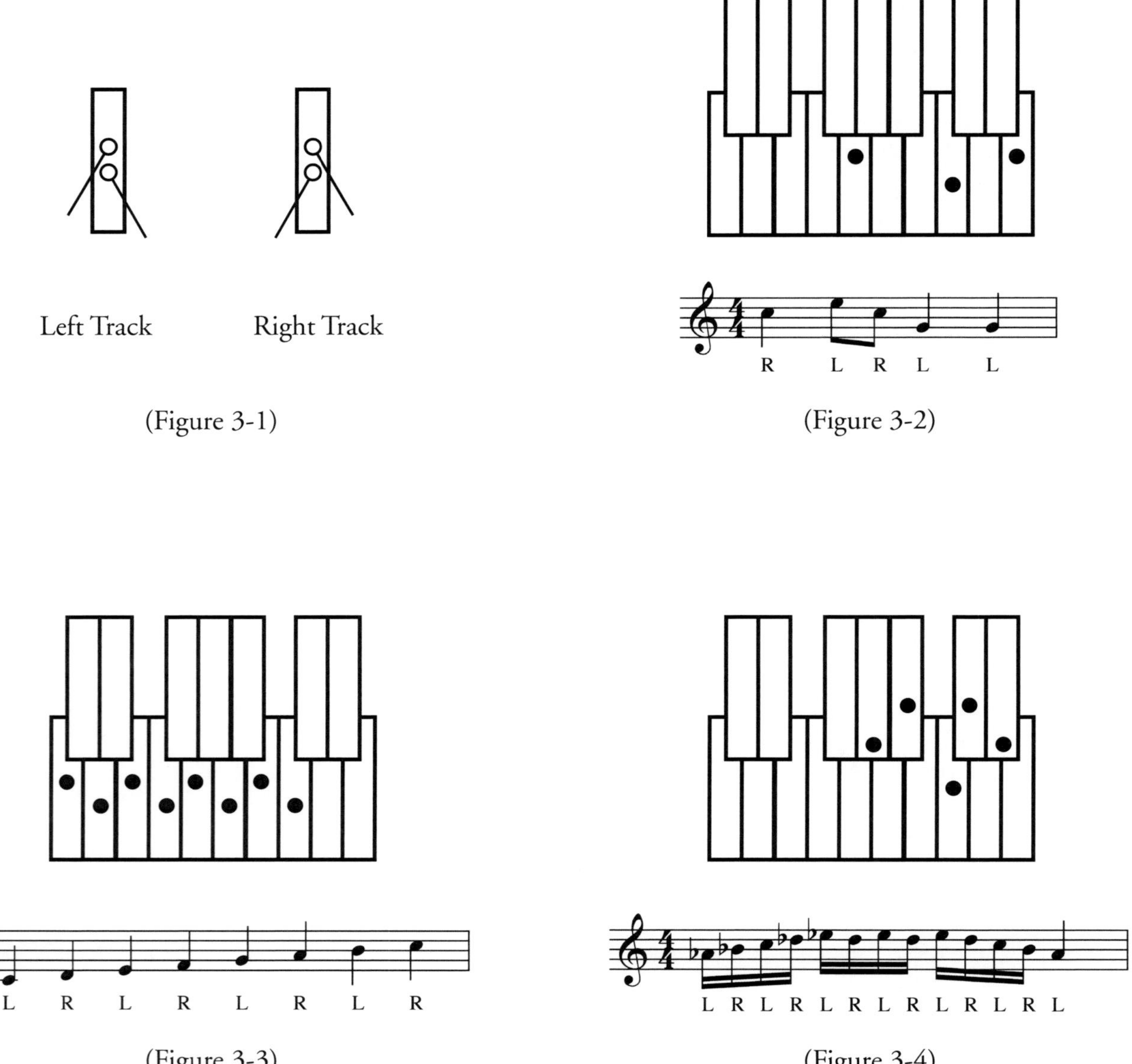

(Figure 3-1)

(Figure 3-2)

(Figure 3-3)

(Figure 3-4)

DISTANCE FROM THE INSTRUMENT

Step-By-Step

1. Face the instrument, as if ready to play.

2. Standing a few feet behind the instrument with weight evenly balanced on both feet and with mallets in hands (Matched Grip – see Chapter 3, p. 32), bend arms at the elbow so that the forearms are parallel to the floor with palms facing down.

3. Elbows should stay in a natural, relaxed position.

4. Without allowing the forearm to move forward or backward in relationship to the body, step toward the instrument and stop the body at the place where the mallet heads rest over the middle of the "natural" bars, equidistant from the nodes (definition of nodes on p. 80). Avoid the tendency to stand too close to the instrument.

5. Place the left mallet over middle "C" and the right mallet over "G" a perfect fifth above using the center of the bar as the playing area (Figure 3-5). Maintain a natural body position, where the elbows remain relaxed. Place both mallets over middle "C" and using the tracking system (p. 82), place the mallets off-center with the left mallet closest to the accidentals. In this position, the mallets should rest over the bar at approximately a 45-degree angle (Fig. 3-6).

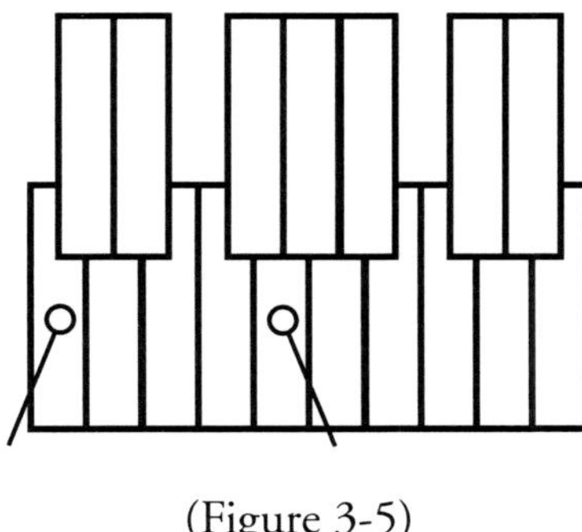

(Figure 3-5)

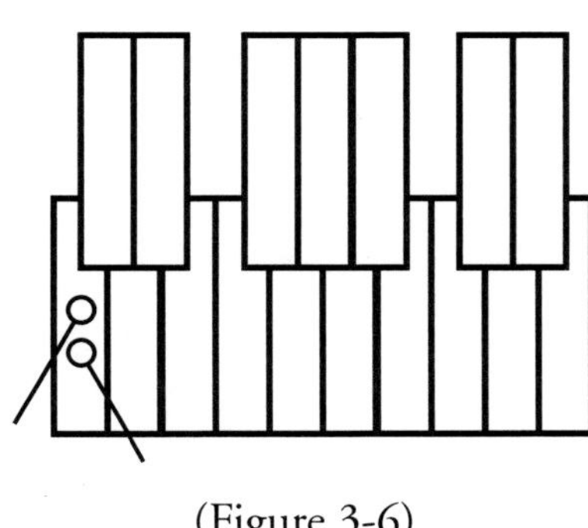

(Figure 3-6)

6. Wrists should be low enough that the knuckles are just above the bars, almost brushing against the bars as the percussionist moves from side to side behind the instrument.

NOTE:

The following discussion of keyboard elements can be divided into two parts: two-mallet and multiple-mallet. The issues associated with two-mallet development will be discussed first, followed by a discussion of multiple-mallet technique.

TWO-MALLET GRIP

Keyboard percussion utilizes the matched grip, as introduced on page 32. The grip should be monitored daily to encourage correct technical development.

TWO-MALLET STRIKING MOTION

The striking motion on keyboard percussion is based on the piston motion discussed in Chapter 1. Piston motion is characterized by a single wrist movement beginning and ending in an up position of predetermined height (determined by dynamic). Although mature percussionists may use some vertical forearm motion in keyboard percussion performance, beginners should use wrist. Keep the following points in mind when developing piston motion on keyboard percussion.

1. There is a correct starting height for every dynamic level. Choose the lowest height that preserves a natural, smooth acceleration of sticks at the proper dynamic. However, do not avoid high motions at loud dynamic levels for fear of loss in accuracy.
    - **Soft Volume** = low stick height with mallet head close to the bar.
    - **Loud Volume** = high stick height with mallet head farther above the bar.
2. The piston motion should be a continuous wrist action, not two separate (up and down) motions. The mallet should return to the highest point of the motion. Each motion ends with the mallet in position to play the next pitch. Avoid wasted motion and multiple preparations!
3. When playing a pitch two or more times consecutively (repeating pitches), the motion is completely vertical.

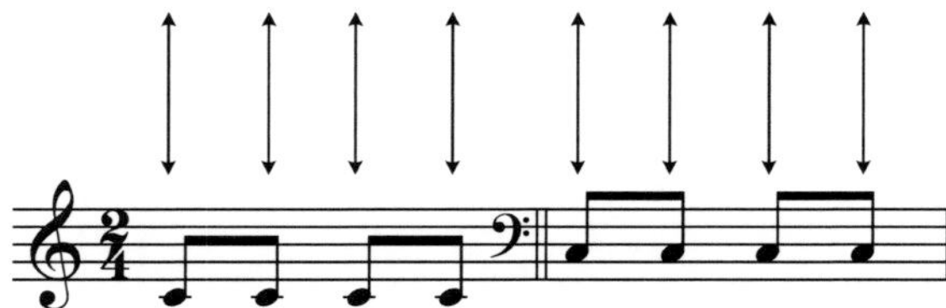

4. When moving from one pitch to another, the following motion is best for beginners because it is efficient and requires no extra motion:
    - The solid arrow represents the "down" part of the motion. The dotted arrow represents the "up" part of the motion. Remember that the piston stroke is one continuous down/up motion, not two separate motions.

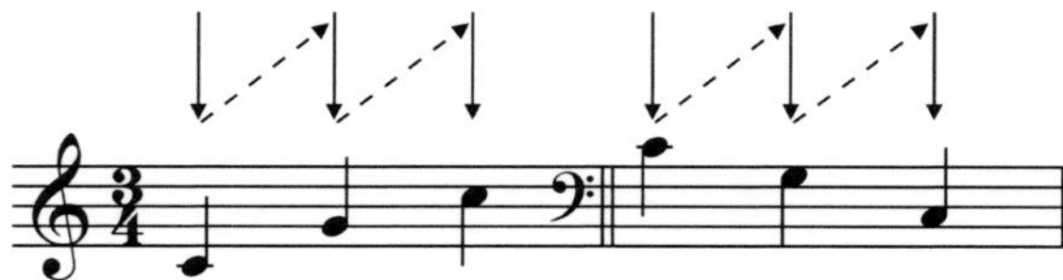

    - No additional preparatory motion is used. Each piston motion should end with the mallet head over the note that the percussionist will play next with that hand, at a stick height that will produce the desired dynamic.

Other methods of moving from one pitch to another may be used by mature keyboard percussionists. However, the movement described above is the one that best coordinates with the Piston Motion and should be taught to beginners as it will serve their needs well into their technical development.

TWO-MALLET STICKING

Refer to multiple-line sticking rules in the Common Elements chapter (Chapter 1).

Step-By-Step

1. Beginners should use alternating whenever possible.

2. If alternating sticking feels awkward, attempt the passage with alternating sticking beginning on the opposite hand.

3. If alternating sticking still feels awkward, isolate the trouble spot and insert a double-sticking that meets the criteria of time and distance sticking rules (Multiple-Line Sticking).

TWO-MALLET ROLLS

Notation: ♩ (with three slashes) ♩ (with tr~~)

Keyboard percussion rolls are produced by alternating single strokes at a speed fast enough to create a sustained sound. Rolls should be played as slow as possible while still achieving a sustained sound. Keep in mind that the contact sound of the mallet hitting the bar is more prevalent when standing at the instrument than it is a few feet away from the instrument. Therefore, always choose the roll speed that achieves a perceived sustained sound from the position of the listener/audience. Avoid using forearm motion when playing rolls. Use wrist.

The higher the pitch	→	**The faster the roll**
The lower the pitch	→	**The slower the roll**
The louder the dynamic	→	**The faster the roll**
The softer the dynamic	→	**The slower the roll**

Keyboard percussion rolls are not as metered as snare drum rolls and are not performed with a conscious rhythmic roll base. However, in order to help develop a smooth roll, it may be beneficial to have the student first perform continuous sixteenth notes moving from pitch to pitch.

Play each pitch as four sixteenth notes at the various tempi given below.

TWO-MALLET ROLLS (cont.)

1. In passages with no accidentals, the right hand should lead when the melodic line ascends and the left hand should lead when the melodic line descends.

2. In passages with accidentals, lead with the hand closest to the next note to be played.

3. Use the most efficient sticking. Do not develop a right hand or left hand lead system in rolled passages making one hand begin all rolls.

4. When playing consecutive rolls, do not stop the motion of the wrists between individually rolled notes. Keep the roll motion going while moving mallet heads over the correct notes. The result is a smoother sounding melodic line.

TEACHING THE TWO-MALLET ROLL

Step-By-Step

1. When the student demonstrates correct piston motion consistently, two-mallet rolls may be introduced.

2. Begin by playing rolls on long tones.

3. Play rolls on step-wise patterns by rote.
   - Use the ear to determine roll speed. Allow the student to explore roll speed by speeding up the roll and slowing down the roll. Then the instructor should guide the student to the most appropriate sustained sound.
   - When playing rolls, monitor piston motion, grip, and body position to make sure that these basic concepts are maintained. During the roll, both mallets must maintain equal stick height!

4. Include the roll in simple reading exercises.

MULTIPLE-MALLET KEYBOARD PERCUSSION

Once the student exhibits consistent execution of piston motion on keyboard percussion instruments with two mallets, four-mallet grip and technique may be introduced. Depending on the student, this may occur almost simultaneously with two-mallet performance. Most beginning multiple-mallet parts will require three mallets (two mallets in one hand, one in the other) or four mallets (two mallet in each hand). Beginning students should hold four mallets, even when a piece calls for three mallets, because it facilitates technical mastery of the grip in a symmetrical manner.

Four-mallet techniques and stroke types should be taught initially by rote. Correct four-mallet form must be well established before attempting to read music while playing for the following reasons:

1. The music reading skills of most students will not be developed to the point of successful multiple-line reading.
2. In the beginning stages of four-mallet development, notation may inhibit technical mastery. A beginning student may be unable to give equal attention to notation and technical development simultaneously. Along with two-mallet technique and reading, the student should begin four-mallet rote exercises that focus on specific stroke types

Multiple-mallet notation is frequently different in appearance from two-mallet notation in that more notes may be struck at one time, multiple staves may be introduced, and the use of both bass and treble clefs (grand staff) becomes more common. Remember that students should learn to read in both clefs from the onset of instruction.

FOUR-MALLET GRIPS

The two types of four-mallet grip are the ***cross grip*** and the ***independent grip***. Each grip has advantages and disadvantages. Many jazz vibraphone players use a type of cross grip because it meets their technical needs. In addition, mastery of the cross grip can be learned more quickly than the independent grip. However, the independent grip is more versatile in achieving overall technical mastery.

In both grips, the mallets may be numbered as follows to make notation of stickings easier.

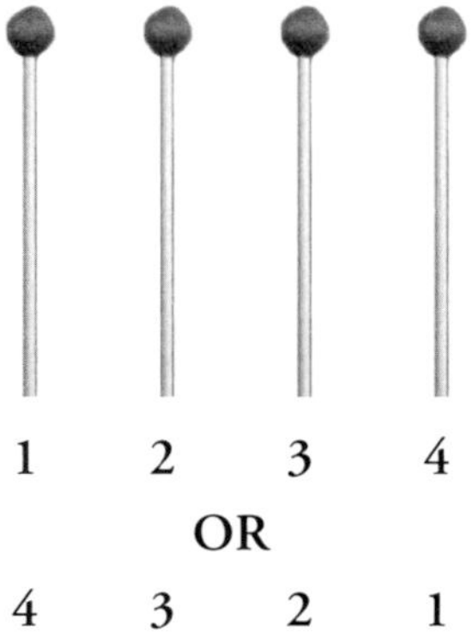

1 2 3 4

OR

4 3 2 1

Inside Mallets: 2 and 3
Outside Mallets: 1 and 4

FOUR-MALLET GRIPS (cont.)

INDEPENDENT GRIP (recommended)

How to Introduce the Independent Grip:
(also referred to as the "Musser Grip" or "Stevens Grip" with slight modifications)

Step-By-Step

The Inside Mallet

1. Position the end of the mallet shaft under the fleshy part of the hand at the base of the thumb.

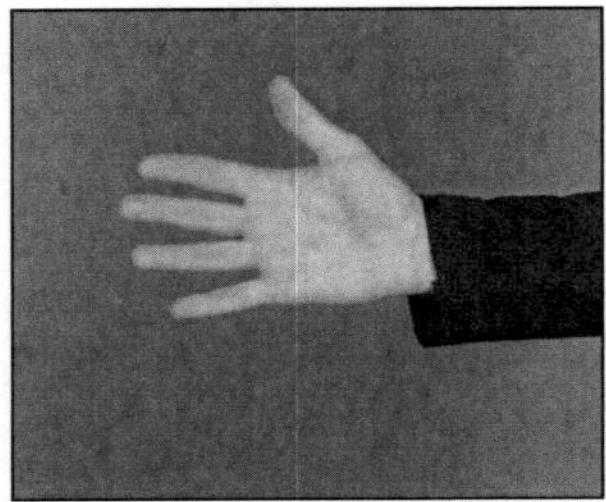

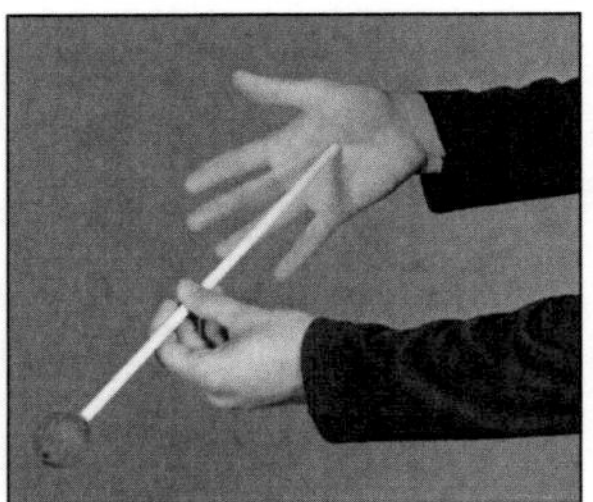

2. Rest the mallet shaft on the first joint of the first finger. A point of balance should occur between the first finger and the base of the thumb.

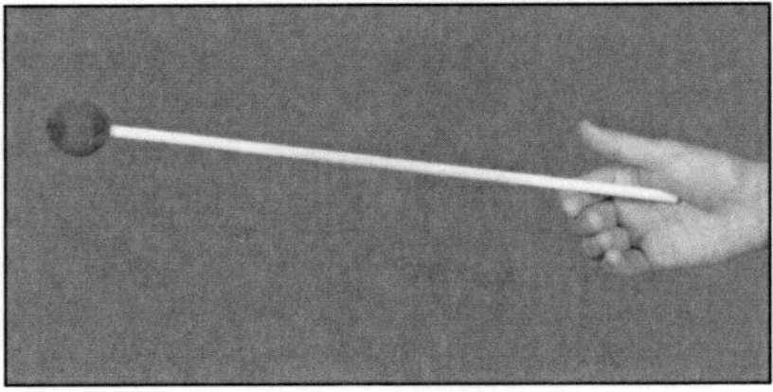

3. Place the thumb on top of the mallet shaft over the first joint of the first finger.

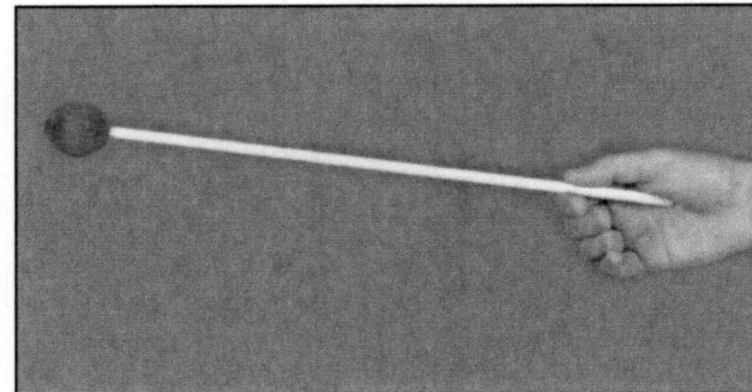

4. Touch the base of the mallet shaft with the middle finger. This finger serves as an "anchor" for the mallet especially during interval changes.

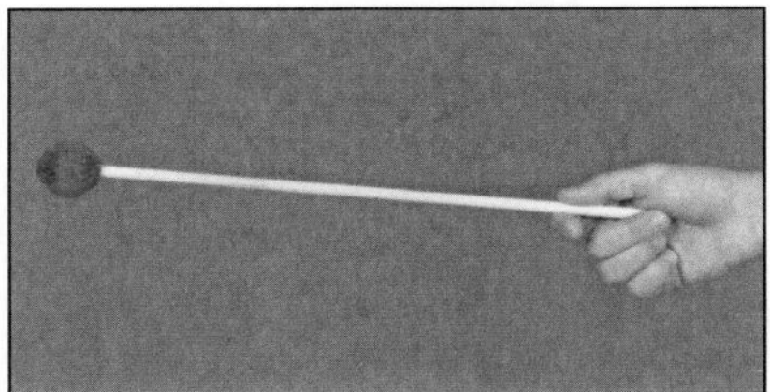

The Outside Mallet

6. The outside mallet is held by the ring and little finger. Place the end of the mallet shaft where the ring and little finger attach to the hand.

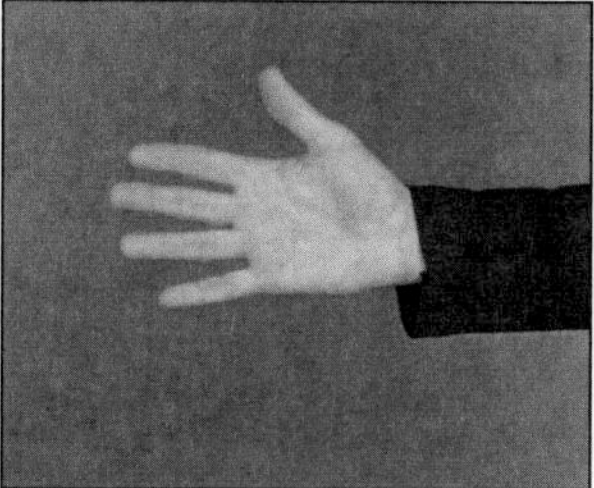

7. Allow the ring and little finger to wrap around the end of the mallet shaft firmly (not tensely).

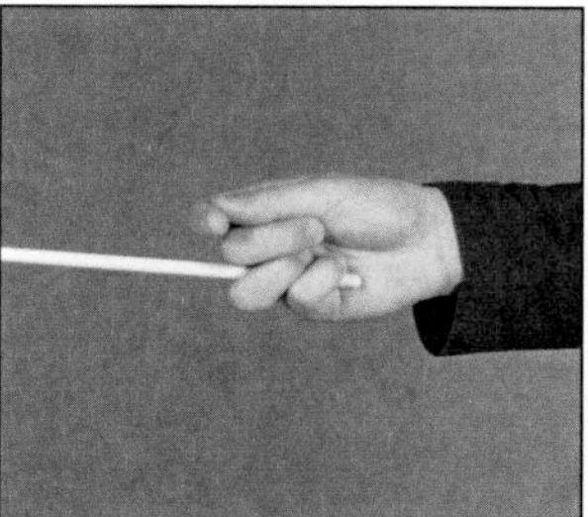

8. In summary, the inside mallet is controlled by the thumb, index finger, and middle finger. The outside mallet is held by the ring and little finger. The top of the thumb faces up and the rest of the fingers will rest in almost a fist position under the thumb. The side of the hand near the little finger will face the floor.

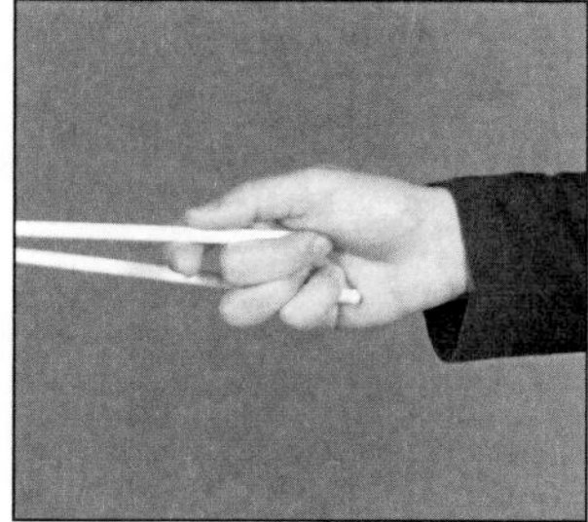

9. The mallet heads should rest at a level position.

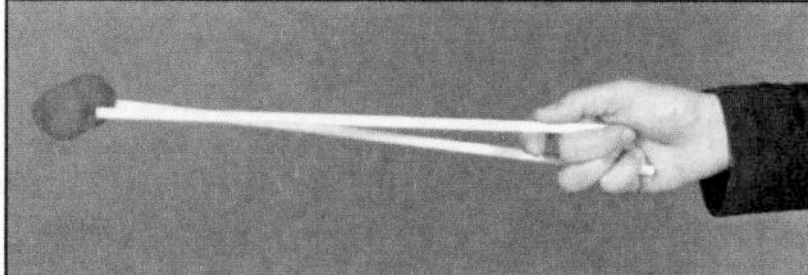

- If the outside mallet droops, check that it has not slipped out of place.
- If the inside mallet points up slightly and rest above the outside mallet, check that the middle finger is touching the shaft of the mallet and that the index finger is extended out farther than the middle finger.

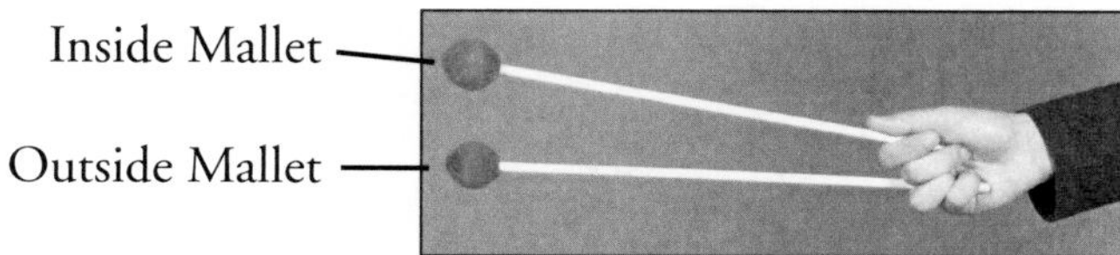

The grip must be carefully monitored on a daily basis, especially in the beginning stages.

FOUR-MALLET GRIPS (cont.)

Interval Changes

10. Interval changes are made by the inside mallet. When changing intervals, the thumb and index finger work together while the middle finger anchors the inside mallet.

    a. To increase interval size, point the index finger out to the side and roll the mallet shaft out with the thumb. In the right hand, the pointing motion will be toward the left with the shaft rolling between the index finger and thumb counterclockwise. The motion will be opposite for the left hand.

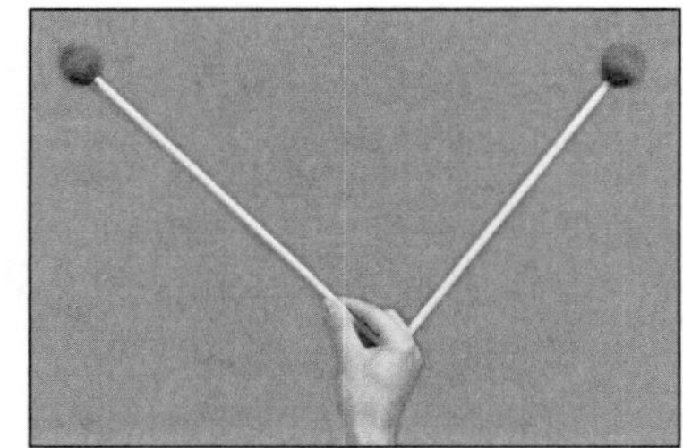

    b. To close an interval, return the index finger toward its original position by rolling the mallet in with the thumb. In the right hand, the shaft will roll clockwise between the index finger and thumb. Remember that the thumb and index finger will work together.

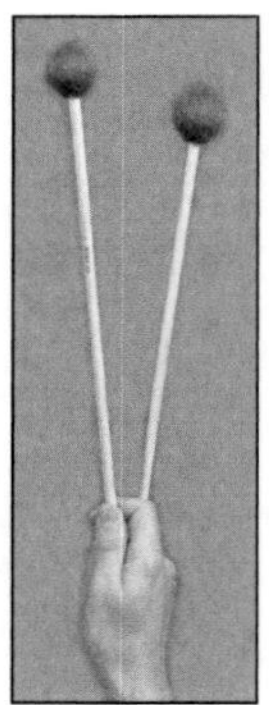

ADVANTAGES OF THE INDEPENDENT GRIP

- The Independent Grip allows for complete independence of each mallet.
- Large and small intervals may be achieved with relative ease. The Independent Grip allows for quick interval changes.
- Because of the variety of stroke types and rolls possible, the grip is very versatile. The versatility of the grip makes it well suited to the technical demands of contemporary percussion literature. (See "Four-Mallet Striking Motion" discussion on page 93 and "Four-Mallet Rolls" discussion on page 97)

SPECIAL CONSIDERATION WHEN USING THE INDEPENDENT GRIP

Because the mallets are held at the very end of the shafts, care should be taken on instruments that require the percussionist to stand close, such as vibraphone. One would need to make sure that the mallet heads were striking in the correct playing area. Shorter mallets could be used to compensate.

CROSS GRIP

How to Introduce the Cross Grip:

(also referred to as the "Traditional Grip," or "Burton Grip" with slight modifications)

Step-By-Step

1. Hold the hand as pictured.

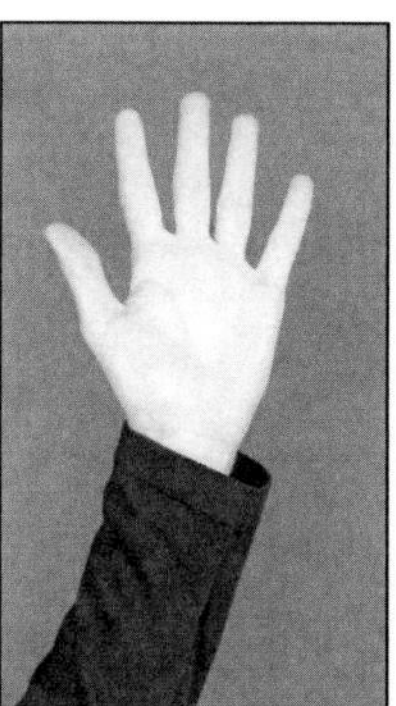

2. Place the mallet shaft between the index and middle finger. This will become the outside mallet.

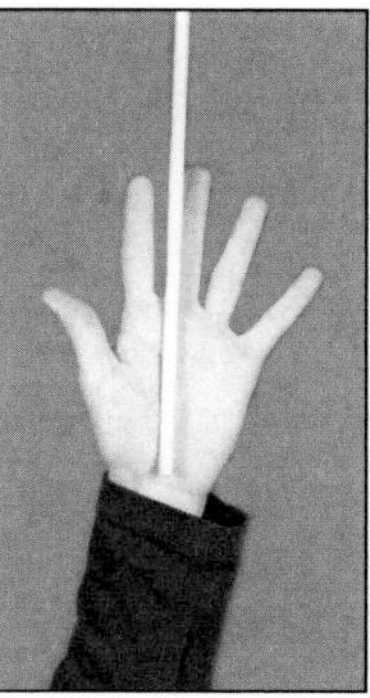

3. Put the other mallet "in the fist" perpendicular to the outside mallet. This creates a 90-degree angle between the two mallets. This becomes the inside mallet.

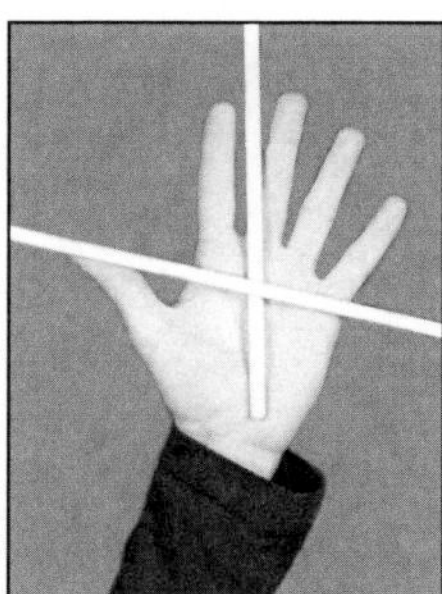

FOUR-MALLET GRIPS (cont.)

4. The inside mallet is held in place by the ring and little finger. The "cross" occurs at the middle finger. The thumb rests on the inside of the inner mallet.

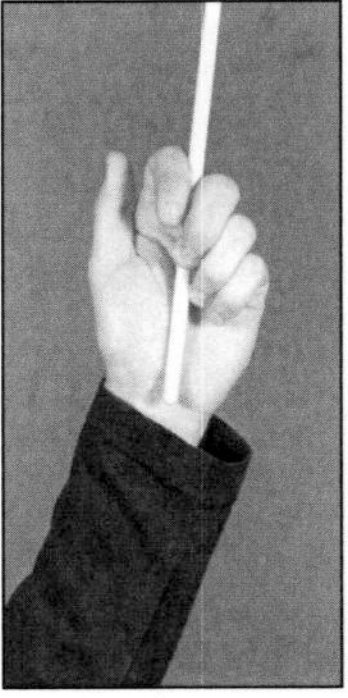

5. The palm then faces the floor.

6. To change intervals, ...

ADVANTAGES OF THE CROSS GRIP

- The strength with which one may perform melodic lines (as in two-mallet literature), coupled with the ability to play block chords, make it well-suited for jazz vibraphone playing.

- Because mallets are not necessarily held at the very end of the shaft, the percussionist may stand closer to the instrument without forcing the mallets into an unsatisfactory playing area. This is important in vibraphone playing because the performer must use the sustain pedal.
- There are fine players that have adapted the cross grip very effectively so that it will have similar advantages to the independent grip.

DISADVANTAGES OF THE CROSS GRIP

- Quick interval changes may be uncomfortable. Also, the fulcrum point is inconsistent when changing intervals because the thumb changes its position upon the inner mallet frequently.

- Large intervals may be difficult because the grip opens comfortably only to a certain point, requiring the thumb to move to the inside of the mallet.

- Small intervals may be difficult because the index finger is positioned between the mallets. For closer intervals, the index finger may be lifted out of the way. However, this temporarily eliminates the fulcrum point.

- Because the mallets "cross" each other, independent movement of any specific mallet is diminished. The result is that independent stroke types are not available or as effective.

FOUR-MALLET STRIKING MOTION
(Independent Grip)

Four stroke types make up most combinations of four-mallet technique. These and other four-mallet stroke motions were identified by Leigh Howard Stevens in his ***Method of Movement.*** The four basic types of strokes that make up independent four-mallet technique are:

Double Vertical
Independent (Outside/Inside)
Alternating Independent
Double Lateral (Outside/Inside)

HOW TO INTRODUCE THE DOUBLE VERTICAL

Step-By-Step

1. Hold two mallets in the right hand. Position the outside mallet over "G" and the inside mallet over "C" below it. Position the mallet heads about 10 inches above the "C" and "G" with the thumb up. Play the interval of a fifth repeatedly without changing pitches. Play slowly enough that correct form is achieved. Make sure that the mallets start and stop in an up position and that both mallets strike the bars at the same time. Practice the right hand, then the left hand, then the right and left hands simultaneously.

2. Maintaining the interval of a fifth, proceed chromatically up and down the keyboard. Play four double vertical strokes per set of pitches. Practice the right hand, then the left hand, and then both hands together.

3. Practice intervals that change from fifths to sixths. Right hand, left hand, and then both hands together. Make the higher pitch adjust the interval the first time through, then make the lower pitch change to adjust the interval the second time through.

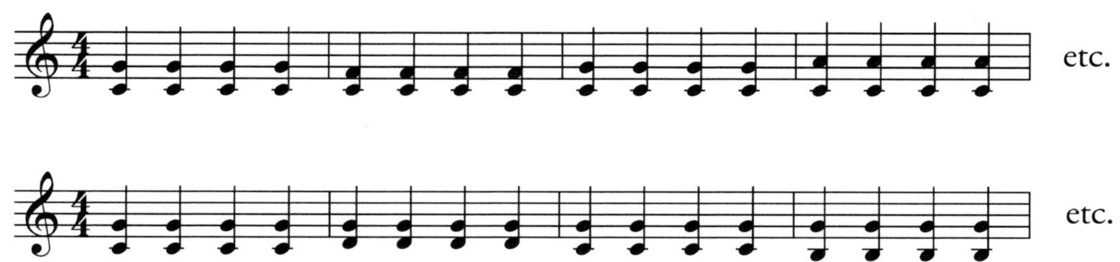

4. Continue with similar exercises that increase and decrease the intervals up to an octave and down to a second. Remember to make the upper pitch change part of the time, and the lower pitch change part of the time.

Note:
Remember to play the exercises at a tempo that allows complete control of correct form. **Form is more important than speed.** Also, remember that the mallet heads must always begin and end in an up position. Once the percussionist is comfortable with playing the exercises at a loud dynamic, the exercises may be practiced at a variety of dynamics by adjusting stick height.

FOUR-MALLET STRIKING MOTION (cont.)

(Independent Grip)

HOW TO INTRODUCE THE INSIDE AND OUTSIDE INDEPENDENT STROKES

A rotating piston motion is used for independent strokes. Individual tones are sounded with each stroke motion. The wrist rotates in a clockwise and counterclockwise motion, like turning a doorknob (rather than an "up and down" motion). It is very important that the mallet return to its original stick height with the rotary motion. The rotation should begin and end in an up position with one motion.

- If the playing mallet ends each stroke in an up position, then the silent mallet will rotate in space as an axis-like pivot point while remaining level with the bars.
- If the playing mallet does not end each motion in an up position, then the silent mallet will begin to move up and down. This increases the possibility of that mallet striking unwanted pitches.

Inside Independent The inside mallet rotates around the outside mallet. The outside mallet forms a stationary axis.

Outside Independent The outside mallet rotates around the inside mallet. The inside mallet forms a stationary axis.

Step-By-Step

1. Practice the inside and outside independent motion, with mallets in hands, away from the instrument.
2. Practice the following exercises at the instrument with attention to the rotary motion of the wrist. The mallet that is performing the stroke should end in an up position ready to perform the next stroke. Keep mallets at the interval of a fourth or fifth. Use the following sequence for all of the exercises below:

   Right Inside, Left Inside, Right Outside, Left Outside, Alternating Right and Left Inside

   a. Practice repeated stroke motions on a single pitch.

   etc.

   b. Practice scalar patterns that move in step-wise motion.

   etc.

   c. Practice patterns that have skips, such as arpeggios or fifths.

   etc.

3. The other exercises in the sequence must be practiced at least an octave apart because of the position of the mallets. Keep mallets at the interval of a fourth or fifth. Use the following sequence for the exercises below: simultaneous right and left inside an octave apart; simultaneous right and left outside; simultaneous left outside and right inside; simultaneous left inside and right outside.

   a. Practice repeated strokes on a single pitch.

   b. Practice scalar patterns that move in step-wise motion.

   c. Practice patterns that have skips, such as arpeggios or fifths.

HOW TO INTRODUCE THE ALTERNATING INDEPENDENT STROKE

The motion used for the alternating independent stroke is a rotating clockwise motion followed by a counter-clockwise motion (or the opposite). The inside and outside mallets in one hand rotate back and forth. Two movements are involved in completing the stroke, resulting in two notes sounding consecutively.

Step-By-Step

Practice the Alternating Independent Stroke, with mallets in hands, away from the instrument. Remember that the Inside/Outside (or Outside/Inside) motion for this stroke is made up of two separate movements. Practice the following exercises with the right hand alone, left hand alone, and both hands simultaneously.

1. Practice the following rhythmic figure in fifths, thirds, and octaves. Move up and down the keyboard chromatically or in a scalar pattern.

2. Practice the following rhythmic figure in fifths, thirds, and octaves.

3. Practice the following rhythmic figure in fifths, thirds, and octaves.

4. Practice the following rhythmic figure in fifths, thirds, and octaves.

FOUR-MALLET STRIKING MOTION (cont.)

(Independent Grip)

HOW TO INTRODUCE THE DOUBLE LATERAL STROKE

The **Double Lateral Stroke** is a single rotating motion that produces two successive pitches (one pitch with the inside and one with the outside mallet). Unlike the alternating independent stroke, the double lateral is only one wrist motion, not two. The rotary motion in the wrist resembles a controlled flicking of the wrist.

Right Hand (Left Hand is opposite):

Clockwise Motion	=	Inside to Outside Motion
Counterclockwise Motion	=	Outside to Inside Motion

Note:
In the double lateral motion, very small intervals are the most difficult because more wrist motion is required when the mallets are closer together.

Step-By-Step

1. Practice the Double Lateral Stroke motion, with mallets in hands, away from the instrument. Remember to give attention to the "flicking" rotary motion of the wrist.

2. When practicing at the instrument, two pitches will sound consecutively (similar to an open flam on snare drum). The wrist makes one smooth motion, not two.

3. Practice the following exercise in fifths, thirds, and octaves. Move up and down the keyboard chromatically or in a scalar pattern.

4. With the Double Lateral Stroke, each motion should end with the mallets prepared over the note or notes that the percussionist will play next with that hand, at a stick height to produce the desired dynamic.

FOUR-MALLET STICKING

(Independent Grip)

Four-mallet sticking patterns incorporate the same general rules as outlined in multiple-line sticking in Chapter 1 and two-mallet sticking (p. 85). However, the process is complicated by having two mallets in each hand.

FOUR-MALLET ROLLS

There are several types of four-mallet rolls. Each roll type offers its own characteristic sound and advantages in specific performance situations. Although additional types of four-mallet rolls are used by mature percussionists, the three types discussed below will meet most of the percussionist's performance needs.

1. **Double Vertical Roll** (sometimes called the hand-to-hand roll)

   This roll uses the alternation of Double Vertical strokes. The hands alternate fast enough to achieve a sustained sound. The speed of the roll should be as slow as possible while maintaining a sustained sound. Remember that the contact sound of the mallet hitting the bar is more prevalent at the instrument than it is a few feet away from the instrument. This roll can be used with both cross and independent grips, and on all types of keyboard percussion instruments.

   - Practice the double vertical roll on long tones and in fifths moving up and down the keyboard chromatically. Use the ear to determine roll speed. **Be careful not to use the forearm. Use wrist motion.**

2. **Double Lateral Roll**

   The Double Lateral Roll consists of alternating Double Lateral strokes (usually outside/inside double lateral strokes). Each of the four mallets hit at different times and each "hit" should be spaced equally.

   One of the advantages of the double lateral roll is that individual mallets may be emphasized (by lifting them higher) for purposes of chord voicing.

   - The student must be able to perform the double lateral stroke before achieving an adequate double lateral roll.

   - First practice the double lateral roll on a flat, unpitched surface (like a table). Give attention to the rotary motion in the wrists.

   - At the instrument, practice the roll in fifths or arpeggios. Move up and down the length of the keyboard chromatically.

3. **Independent Rolls** (sometimes called the one-handed roll)

   In the Independent Roll, the inside and outside mallets in one hand alternate back and forth with a smooth rotary motion. It is similar to the Alternating Independent stroke. However, instead of the motion being two separate rotating motions, it is one continuous back and forth rotary motion. The motion must be smooth and consistent. Even stick height between the mallets must be observed for an even sound.

   - Independent rolls may be played in both hands at the same time with like or different roll speeds. Perhaps the most important use of independent rolls is to allow pitch to be sustained with one hand, while other musical ideas are performed with the other hand.

FOUR-MALLET ROLLS (cont.)

Independent Rolls (cont.)

Step-By-Step

1. Practice the Independent Roll in intervals of fifths, thirds, and octaves.

   Exercise 1: Use the following rhythmic figure (practice beginning on both the inside and outside mallet)

   Exercise 2: Use the following rhythmic figure (practice beginning on both the inside and outside mallet)

   Exercise 3: Practice the Independent Roll, without a break in the motion, for given lengths of time, gradually increasing the length of the roll (5 seconds, 10 seconds, 15 seconds, etc.). **Allow time to develop the roll.**

2. Practice each hand separately, then both hands together.

3. Use the exercises listed under "Alternating Independent Stroke" (p. 95). However, keep the wrist motion smooth and continuous. The roll should not be divided up into separate strokes.

WHEN AND HOW TO BEGIN KEYBOARD PERCUSSION

Students should play keyboard percussion instruments, along with snare drum, at the onset of instruction. In a heterogeneous setting, keyboard percussion instruments may be used in the following manner:

- Participate in warm-up activities with wind instruments. For example, the keyboard percussion instruments could play scalar and arpeggiated figures while wind players are playing complementary warm-up figures (scales or long tones).

- Perform from a band class method with other wind and percussion instruments (keyboard percussion book, oboe book, etc.).

WHEN AND HOW TO BEGIN KEYBOARD PERCUSSION (cont.)

Sample Lesson 1

1. Point out the arrangement of "accidental" bars on the instrument (in groups of two and three like a piano keyboard). Using "accidental" notes as a guide, have students find all of the "Cs" or "Fs" on the keyboard. Other notes could be used. Note identification on the instrument is the important goal.

2. Teach matched grip and piston motion.

3. Practice piston motion on repeated single pitches, such as "C" and "F." Have students echo a rhythm clapped to them. First perform this with the right hand, then with the left hand, then alternating.

4. Demonstrate body position and playing area.

5. Experiment with tone color and make choices about where bars should be struck for the best tone.

   For example:
   On the pitch "F," begin striking the bar repeatedly at the extreme edge and continue striking as you move to the center of the bar. Then move back out to the extreme edge. Discuss the differences in tone.

   Teach the first five pitches of the "F" scale by rote. Have the student:

   - Play up and down the five-note scale in the center of the bar.
   - Play just off center of the bar.
   - Play the B-flat within the scale on the extreme edge of the bar.
   - Play the B-flat within the scale on the node.

   Discuss the differences in tone throughout the exploration. Bell kits are more limited in playing area because of bar size. This exercise is better suited for a full-size instrument.

6. By rote, practice piston motion with scalar patterns. First practice the right hand, then the left, then alternating. Remember that the motion should always end with the mallet head in an up position over the next note it will play. These exercises should include the entire length of the keyboard. When moving behind the instrument, move feet in a side-step "shuffle" manner. Do not cross one foot over or behind the other. Continually keep the body centered in relationship to the passage of notes being played.

WHEN AND HOW TO BEGIN KEYBOARD PERCUSSION (cont.)

Sample Lesson 2

7. Review all activities in Lesson 1.

8. By rote, practice piston motion with melodic patterns with skips (such as arpeggios or fifths). Practice hands separately, then together. The mallet heads should always end in an up position over the bar to be played next. These exercises should include the entire length of the instrument.

   The amount of movement required as the student moves up and down the length of the instrument is dependent on the size of the instrument. Because orchestra bells, or student bell kits, have a smaller range and bar size, little movement is required. Xylophones and marimbas have a larger range and bar size and, therefore, require more movement. Remember to move the feet in a side-step "shuffle" manner. Do not cross one foot over or behind the other.

9. Assuming that the student has learned to read several pitches, read simple melodies (beginning with 2 or 3 pitches) that move step-wise. Keep the music stand down so that the bottom of the stand is level with the keyboard. **The student must keep his/her eyes on the MUSIC, not the bars.** Peripheral vision may be used to see both the music and the instrument, but moving the head and eyes back and forth from the music to the bars should be avoided. Kinesthetic memory related to how far one must move between notes will develop with consistent practice (see performance issues on p. 105). Monitor piston motion closely and encourage alternating sticking.

Sample Lesson 3

10. Review all previous activities.

11. Read simple melodies using alternating sticking. Monitor piston motion. Do not allow the student to look down at the bars.

12. Continue this sequence by involving the students in instrumental activities that further develop their reading skills, listening skills, technical skills, and musicianship. Monitor the grip daily and make sure that the students look at the music, not the bars, while reading.

TEACHING FOUR-MALLET TECHNIQUE

When the student demonstrates the correct piston motion using two mallets (one mallet in each hand) and two-mallet rolls consistently, then the four-mallet sequence may be introduced by rote.

Sample 15-Minute Lesson 1

1. Introduce the Independent Grip as shown on p. 88. Experiment with changing intervals away from the instrument by moving the inside mallet back and forth.

2. At the instrument, experiment with playing intervals, especially fourths and fifths, by moving the inside mallet back and forth.

3. Introduce the Double Vertical Stroke as shown on p. 93. One can spend as much time as needed practicing Lesson 1 before moving to Lesson 2. **Establishing proper form is very important.**

Sample Lesson 2

4. Review all exercises above.

5. When the student demonstrates a correct Double Vertical Stroke, introduce the Inside and Outside Independent Strokes as shown on p. 94. Spend as much time practicing the aforementioned stroke types before adding others. **Form is very important.**

Sample Lesson 3

6. Review all exercises above.

7. When the student demonstrates a correct Double Vertical Stroke and Inside/Outside Independent Stroke, introduce the Alternating Independent Stroke as shown on p. 95. Spend as much time as needed practicing all of the above stroke types so that they become comfortable. These stroke types will form the basis of future four-mallet technique.

8. Continue the sequence by practicing all of the above stroke types in similar exercises.

Sample Lesson 4

9. Review all exercises above.

10. When the student demonstrates correct form with the above stroke types, introduce the Double Vertical Roll.
    - Practice on long tones, such as fermata notes directed by the instructor of whole notes.
    - Make sure that both hands are using equal stick height. Use the ear to determine sustained sound. Experiment with speeding up and slowing down the roll speed in different registers of the instrument

11. Continue the development of the roll with similar exercises. The Double Lateral Stroke, Double Lateral Roll, and Independent Roll should be introduced when the student needs those techniques in the literature he/she is performing

MALLET SELECTION

Tone, timbre, and articulation are influenced by mallet selection. Each different keyboard percussion instrument requires specific types of mallets. The mallet is made up of two parts: the mallet head and the shaft.

Mallet Head
The inner part of the mallet head is called the core. The core is usually made of rubber or hard plastic.

- **Wound Mallets:** If the core is wrapped with such material as yarn, cord, or latex, it is referred to as a wound mallet. Wound mallets are used on marimba and vibraphone.

- **Unwound Mallets:** If the core is left unwrapped, it is referred to as an unwound mallet. Unwound mallets are usually made of rubber, hard plastic, nylon, or wood. Unwound mallets are used on bells and xylophone.

Mallet Shafts
Mallet shafts are made out of rattan, wood, or fiberglass.

- **Rattan:** Rattan is flexible and especially useful for two-mallet playing, although it tends to warp.

- **Birch:** Birch shafts are especially useful for four-mallet independent grip playing because they are long and straight. Birch shafts are not as likely to warp as rattan.

- **Fiberglass:** The characteristic look of fiberglass shafts (sometimes called "two-step") is a white shaft that becomes thinner between the middle of the shaft and the mallet head.

Except for instruments with metal bars, the range of the instrument may influence mallet selection. The following are general rules:

The **lower the pitch** and **softer the dynamic**, the **softer and heavier the mallet.**

The **higher the pitch** and **louder the dynamic**, the **harder and lighter the mallet.**

The hardness/articulation of a wound mallet depends upon the hardness and/or weight of the core and how tightly the yarn or other material surrounding the core is wrapped.

Hard core and tight wrap = Articulate mallet (loud or upper register)

Softer core and loose wrap = Less articulate mallet (soft or lower register)

A medium weight core with a medium tight wrap will sound good throughout the instrument range (a medium multi-purpose mallet).

NEVER STRIKE AN INSTRUMENT WITH A MALLET THAT IS HARDER THAN THE BAR

CHARACTERISTICS OF KEYBOARD PERCUSSION INSTRUMENTS

All of the keyboard percussion instruments are arranged in the same manner as a piano keyboard.

ORCHESTRA BELLS (Glockenspiel)

It is common for composers to write out of the range of the orchestra bells. In that case, adjust the octave so that the notes fit on the instrument.

Bars:	Steel Alloy or Aluminum (Steel is preferred)
Range:	2-1/2 to 3 Octaves
Sounding:	2 Octaves Higher Than Written
Mallets:	Hard Plastic, Rubber

Written Range

STUDENT BELL KIT

Bars:	Aluminum
Range:	1-1/2 Octaves
Sounding:	2 Octaves Higher Than Written
Mallets:	Hard Plastic, Rubber

Written Range

XYLOPHONE

Because of the tuning of the instrument, the resonators are shorter than those on a marimba and the timbre is brighter with less resonance.

Bars:	Rosewood or Synthetic Material
Range:	3-1/2 Octaves
Sounding:	1 Octave Higher Than Written
Mallets:	Hard Plastic, Nylon, Rubber

VIBRAPHONE

Bars:	Aluminum Alloy
Range:	3 to 4 Octaves
Sounding:	As Written
Mallets:	Yarn, Cord

Vibraphone bars rest on a pedal-controlled damper similar to the sustain pedal on a piano. When the pedal is depressed, the bars ring or sustain. When the pedal is released, the bars are dampened. Specific bars may be dampened with a finger or mallet.

A metal disc is located at the top of each resonator, where it is controlled by an electric motor. The motor turns the discs and the tone produced has a vibrato sound. This vibrato is only heard when the sustain pedal is down so the bars can ring. The speed of the vibrato may be controlled by the motor as well. Often the vibraphone is played without the motor on. In that case, the discs should be turned so that the resonators are open at the top.

The vibraphone is capable of producing many special effects because of the sustaining capabilities of the instrument and the metal bars. For example, the vibraphone can be played with a bass bow or "pitch bending" may be performed with a hard mallet. Care should be taken to play in the correct playing area for full resonance. For further information concerning vibraphone performance techniques, see "Performance Issues" on p. 105.

CHARACTERISTICS OF KEYBOARD PERCUSSION INSTRUMENTS (cont.)

MARIMBA

Bars:	Rosewood (preferred) or Synthetic Material
Range:	See Below
Sounding:	As Written
Mallets:	Yarn, Cord

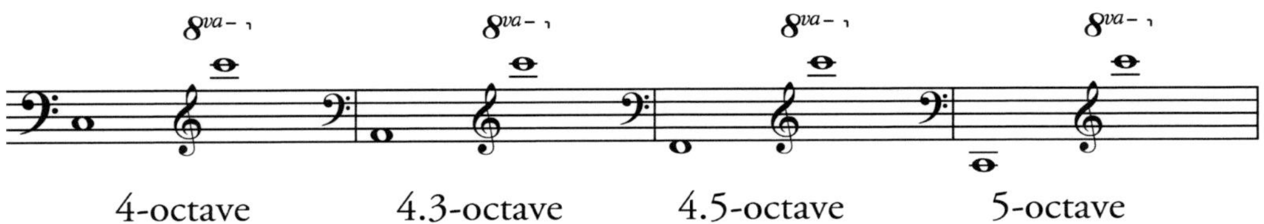

Rosewood bars produce a more characteristic marimba sound than do synthetic bars.

CHIMES (Tubular Bells)
A sustaining pedal is attached to the instrument frame to control the duration of instrument resonance. At the top of each chime is a "cap." The side of this cap is the appropriate striking area. Striking the chimes in any other area will result in damage to the instrument.

Bars:	Brass Tubes (1-1/2 inch)
Range:	1-1/2 Octaves
Sounding:	As Written
Mallets:	Rawhide, Plastic, or Acrylic Hammers

Written Range

KEYBOARD PERCUSSION PERFORMANCE SKILLS IN A HETEROGENEOUS INSTRUMENTAL CLASS

Keyboard percussion skills should begin at the onset of instruction. Otherwise, it is less likely to develop to the students' fullest potential. Use the aforementioned teaching sequence to teach beginning keyboard percussion. Those same activities may be used for older beginners. However, the pace of activities might need to be adjusted for students with more developed coordination and attention span.

HOW TO MAINTAIN KEYBOARD SKILLS

1. Rotate so that all students play a keyboard instrument every day (or at least every other day for older students).
2. Use as many keyboard percussion instruments as possible in activities such as warm-up, etudes, and playing music.
3. Double wind parts from the instrumental ensemble on keyboard percussion instruments. Not only will it help to maintain keyboard percussion skills, but it can strengthen the wind sound as well, especially if mallet choice and timbre are considered.
4. Involve the percussionists in percussion ensemble literature that incorporates keyboard percussion parts.
5. Have the students perform solos or etudes on keyboard percussion instruments.
6. **Always emphasize the Common Elements.**

PERFORMANCE ISSUES UNIQUE TO KEYBOARD PERCUSSION INSTRUMENTS

1. Although there are similarities between the different keyboard percussion instruments, there are many differences as well. Frequently, educators make the mistake of assuming that students can switch from one keyboard instrument to another easily. While students should be able to play all keyboard instruments, it takes a few minutes for students to become oriented to the new keyboard. Remember that not all of the keyboard instruments are the same. Factors such as bar size and feel of the mallet on the bar affect performance. The more practice students have on a variety of instruments, the fewer problems they will have and the quicker they will adjust.

2. An issue in keyboard percussion performance not faced in any other melodic instruments centers around reading music. Because the percussionist never touches the instrument physically, a sense of kinesthetic memory must be developed. If the performer looks at the bars continually, it is extremely difficult to keep one's place in the music. The performer MUST looks at the music, not bars, while reading. Keeping the music stand near the bars allows for the use of peripheral vision. Kinesthetic memory, or "knowing the keyboard," may be developed only through practice. Frequent sight-reading and exercises performed without looking at the bars help to develop these skills. Changing from one keyboard percussion instrument to a different keyboard instrument influences kinesthetic memory drastically. Educators must be aware of such issues so that appropriate skills are developed.

3. There are a few techniques that are unique to vibraphone playing.

    - If the sustain pedal is not depressed, then the tone will be short and muffled.

    - If the sustain pedal is depressed, then the notes will ring until the pedal is released. Release of the pedal stops the sustain of all notes. Pedaling is one way of controlling harmony and phrasing on the vibraphone.

    - If the player wants some of the tones to be dampened while others are left to ring, then the pedal should remain depressed while individual notes are dampened with a finger or a mallet.

    - Dampening notes with the mallet or hand while the pedal is down may allow for a smoother sounding line than pedaling each individual note. One note must be dampened at the same time the next note is played.

SELECT KEYBOARD PERCUSSION RESOURCES

Methods/Collections

The Book of Percussion Audition Music	N. Daughtrey/C. McClaren	C. Alan Publications, LLC
Five Easy Two-Mallet Pieces for Marimba	J. Metzger	C. Alan Publications, LLC
Five Pieces for Vibraphone	J. Metzger	C. Alan Publications, LLC
Fundamental Studies for Mallets	G. Whaley	Meredith Music Publications
Four-Mallet Marimba Playing	N. Zeltsman	Hal Leonard
Method of Movement for Marimba	L.H. Stevens	Keyboard Percussion Publications

Solos

Challenge I	E. Hatch	Studio 4 Music
Classic Suite for Marimba	G. Zyskowski	C. Alan Publications, LLC
Funny Mallet Series	N. Zivkovic	Gretel-Verlag
Mountain Paths	N. Daughtrey	C. Alan Publications, LLC
Of Thoughts and Thinking	A. Lymon	C. Alan Publications, LLC
Vibraphone Technique: Pedaling & Dampening	D. Friedman	Berklee Press Publications

Chapter 6

ACCESSORY INSTRUMENTS

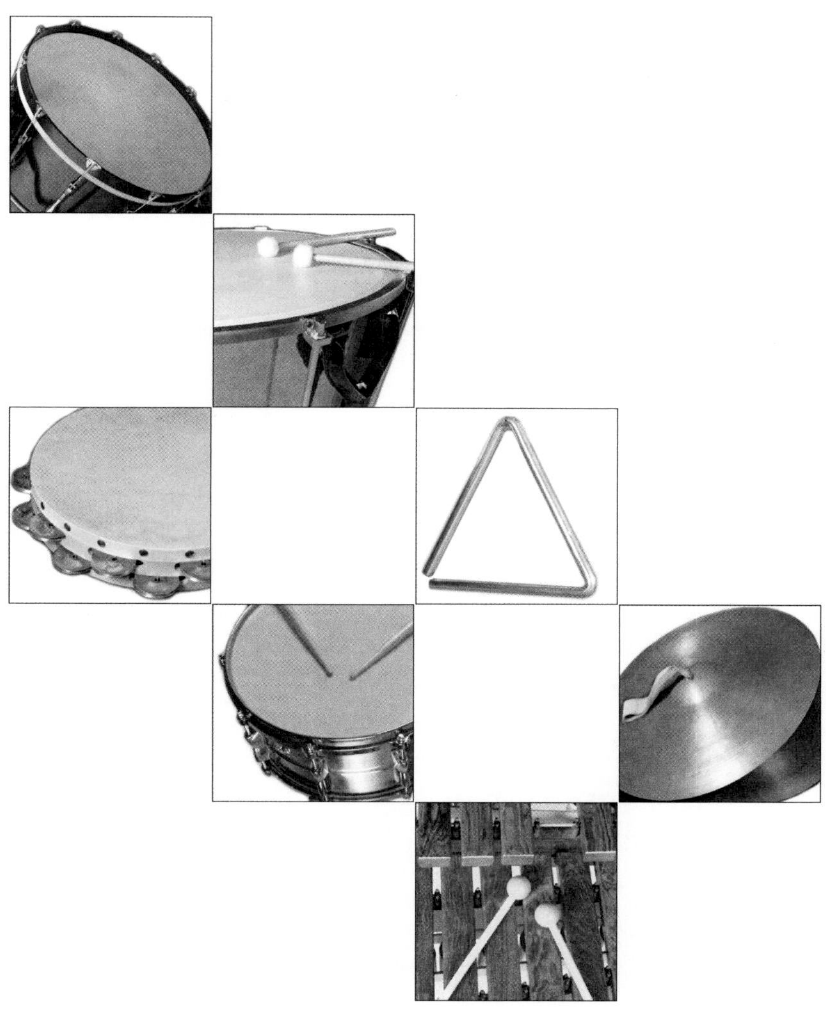

Chapter 5

ACCESSORY INSTRUMENTS

BASS DRUM

The Common Elements

Posture
Grip
Striking Motion
Volume
Sticking
Rolls

POSTURE

The correct posture for general purpose concert bass drum playing is provided below. This process assumes that the player is playing with his/her right hand.

Step-By-Step

1. Imagine a line that runs vertically down the middle of the body, dividing the body in half.

2. Stand 3 to 4 feet from the bass drum while facing the shell. Align the imaginary line down the center of the body with the hoop of the "playing side" of the bass drum.

3. With a mallet in the right hand, bend the arm at the elbow so that the forearm is parallel to the floor.

4. Walk toward the bass drum and stop when the mallet head is over the proper playing area (See playing area below).

5. The player should be able to tilt the bass drum slightly for executing passages that require two mallets. However, avoid placing the bass drum on its side to play rolls or difficult passages. The bass drum is a directional instrument and placing it on its side will alter the way in which the sound reaches the audience.

PLAYING AREA

The batter head will be to the player's right (if playing primarily with the right hand). Playing area for general purpose playing is slightly off center.

HEIGHT

Suspended and tilting bass drum stands are not height adjustable, although their height should accommodate most players. Folding or cradle-style bass drum stands are height adjustable and, for this reason, are recommended for younger players.

GRIP

Step-By-Step

1. Hold the bass drum mallet using matched grip.

2. Turn hand so that the thumb faces the ceiling.

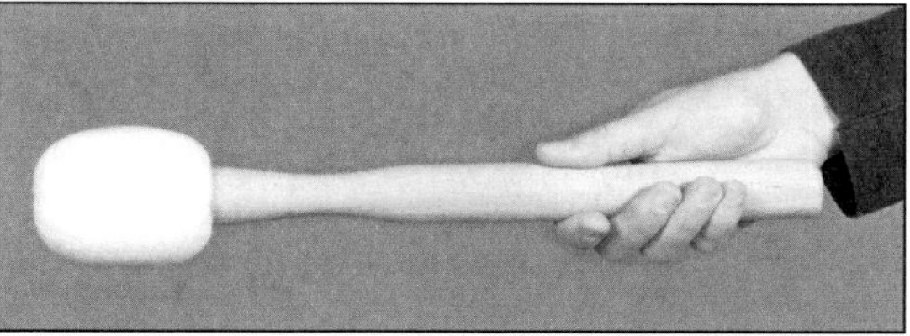

STRIKING MOTION

Piston Motion is used in bass drum playing, as in all other percussion instrument playing. However, instead of a vertical motion (as in snare drum), horizontal motion is used in playing bass drum. The horizontal piston motion used for the bass drum can be envisioned by turning the hand sideways (thumb on top) and waving the hand back and forth. The stroke is played directly into the drum. Avoid a circular motion or a glancing blow.

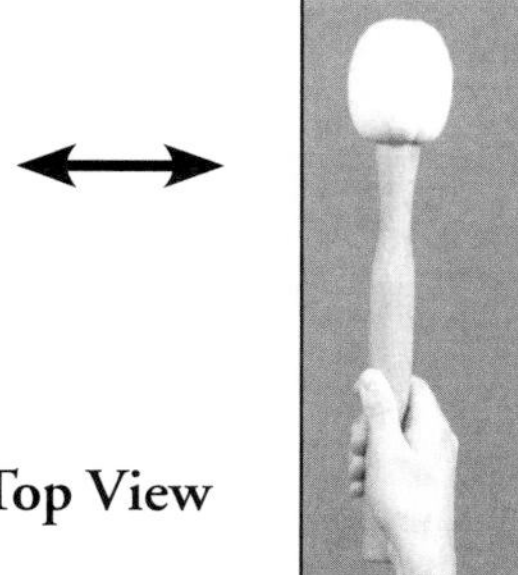

Top View

VOLUME

Distance between the mallet and the drum head will determine volume.

STICKING

The bass drum is ordinarily played with one mallet. Use two identical mallets in more difficult passages and for rolls.

ROLLS

Single stroke (alternating motion) rolls with two identical mallets are used on bass drum. A sustained sound (or a roll) is achieved with a pair of matched bass drum mallets by striking the drum at either the two o'clock and four o'clock positions or the twelve o'clock and six o'clock positions. Each mallet should be equidistant from the center.

The bass drum may be tilted slightly to accommodate the left hand.

Mallets at 2 O'Clock and 4 O'Clock

Mallets at 12 O'Clock and 6 O'Clock

MINIMUM BASS DRUM SKILLS FOR HIGH SCHOOL GRADUATES

		Student Names			
Skill 1.	Demonstrate a sixteen-beat roll at quarter note = 100, starting ***pp*** and ending at ***ff*** using appropriate roll speed.				
Skill 2.	Demonstrate sixteenth notes at quarter note = 120 using two mallets.				
Skill 3.	Demonstrate correct muffling technique with the other hand while playing ***pp*** half notes at quarter note = 100.				
Skill 4.	Perform a ***sforzando*** cannon shot. Let ring for four beats at quarter note = 120, then dampen using appropriate dampening technique.				
Skill 5.	Perform bass drum etude on following page.				

MINIMUM BASS DRUM SKILLS FOR HIGH SCHOOL GRADUATES (cont.)

Skill #1

Demonstrate a sixteen-beat roll at quarter note = 100, starting ***pianissimo*** and ending at ***fortissimo*** using appropriate roll speed.

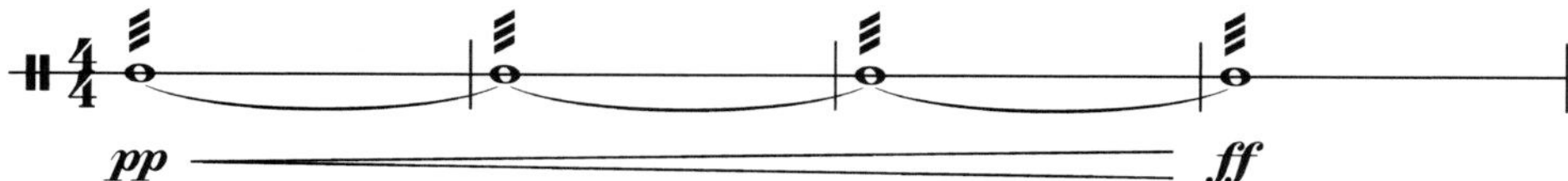

Skill #2

Demonstrate sixteenth notes at quarter note = 120 using two mallets.

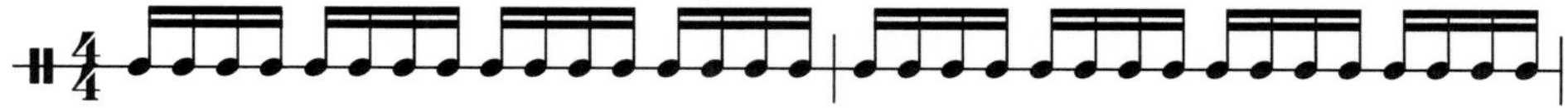

Skill #3

Demonstrate correct muffling technique while playing ***pianissimo*** half notes at quarter note = 100.

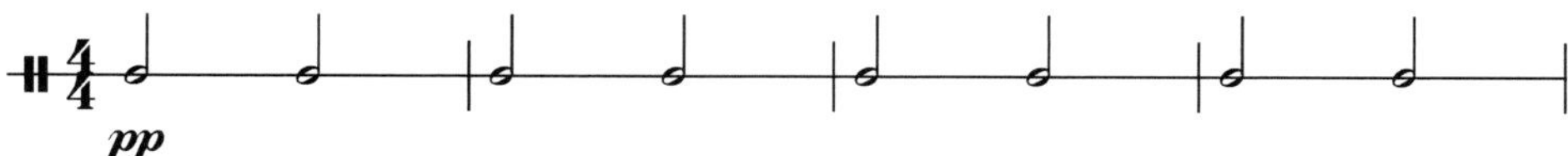

Skill #4

Perform a ***sforzando*** cannon shot. Let ring for four beats at quarter note = 120, then dampen using appropriate dampening technique.

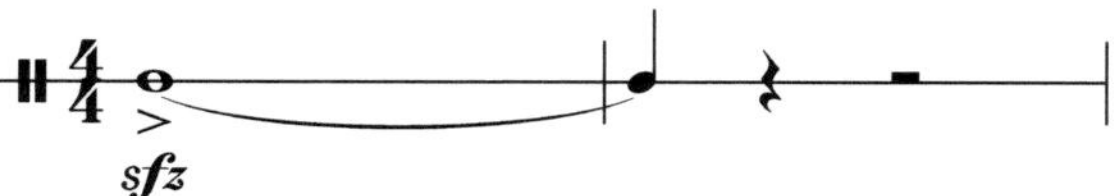

Skill #5

Perform etude below.

Bass Drum Etude

CRASH CYMBALS

The Common Elements

Posture
Grip
Striking Motion
Volume
Sticking
Rolls

POSTURE

Stand straight with feet slightly apart and body weight evenly balanced.

GRIP

Each cymbal is held with the matched grip, similar to holding snare drum sticks. Refer to Step 3 under "General Purpose Crash" on the next page.

STRIKING MOTION

Piston Motion (see Chapter 1) is applicable to crash cymbals.

VOLUME

The distance between two crash cymbals will determine the volume of a given crash.

GENERAL PURPOSE CRASH

Step-By-Step

1. The cymbal player must have a padded table large enough to hold two crash cymbals side by side.

2. Place two crash cymbals side by side on a padded table with ends of the straps facing the performer.

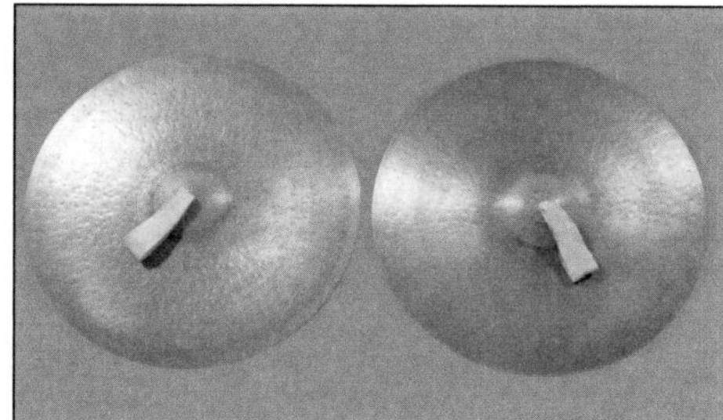

3. Imagine holding a pair of snare drum sticks using matched grip. Grasp the cymbal straps as if picking up snare drum sticks with the fulcrum near the bell of the cymbal.

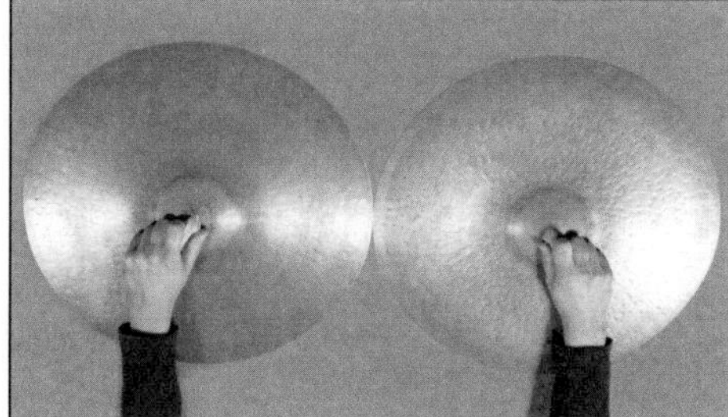

4. Raise both cymbals and hold them perpendicular to the table. Rest the bottom edges on the table.

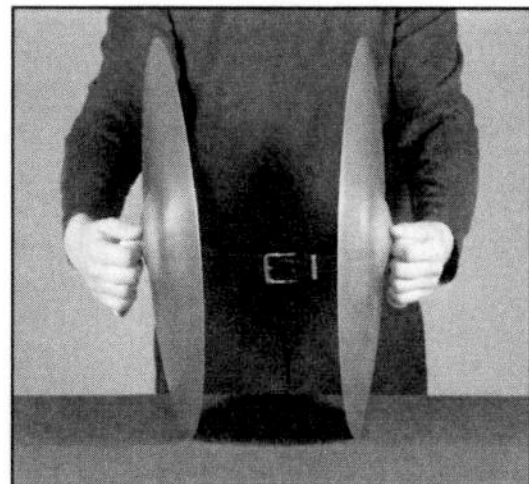

5. Lift the cymbals off the table slightly and gently tap the bottom edge of each cymbal on the padded table. This will cause the two cymbals to vibrate. There is some debate over what, if any, effect this has on the sound quality of the crash. Therefore, this step is optional.

GENERAL PURPOSE CRASH (cont.)

6. Keeping the cymbals parallel with one another, turn them to a slight angle to the performer's body, with the left cymbal on bottom and the right cymbal on top. Adjust the cymbals so the performer can see approximately 3/4 inch of the bottom cymbal.

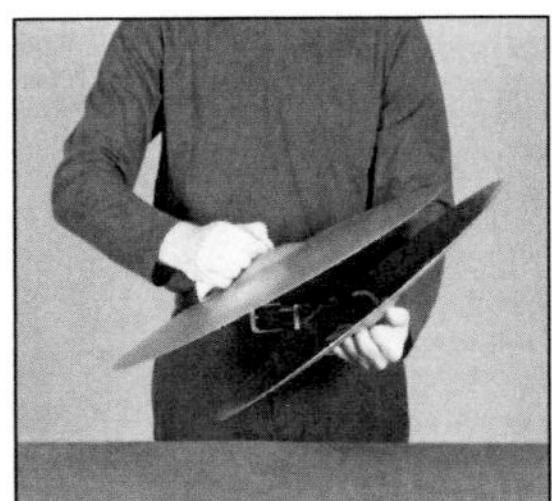

7. For a *mf* crash, raise the top cymbal approximately 6 inches above the bottom cymbal. Keep in mind that the distance between cymbals determines the volume of a crash.

8. Using piston motion, drop the top cymbal into the bottom cymbal to achieve a crash and return the top cymbal to its starting position (ready to move immediately to Step 9). Always drop the top cymbal directly into the bottom cymbal, keeping the edges of the cymbals offset approximately 3/4 inch. Never slide one cymbal across another while crashing. Doing so will cause an air pocket (undesirable sound).

9. After the crash, the performer has the following choices:

   A. Hold the cymbals parallel to each other, slightly separated.
   B. Separated the cymbals in a suspended fashion, holding each with the inside of the cymbal facing the floor.

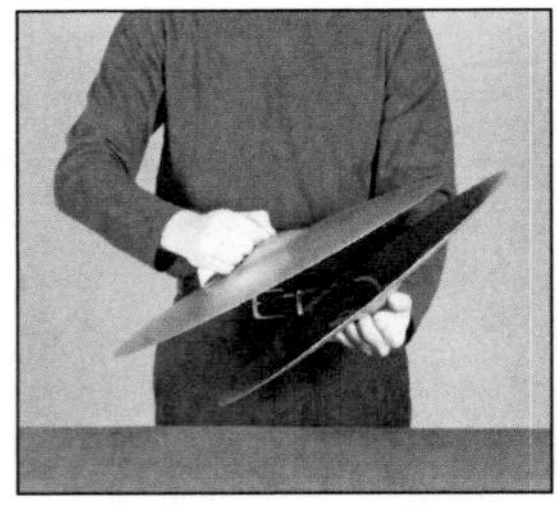

A.

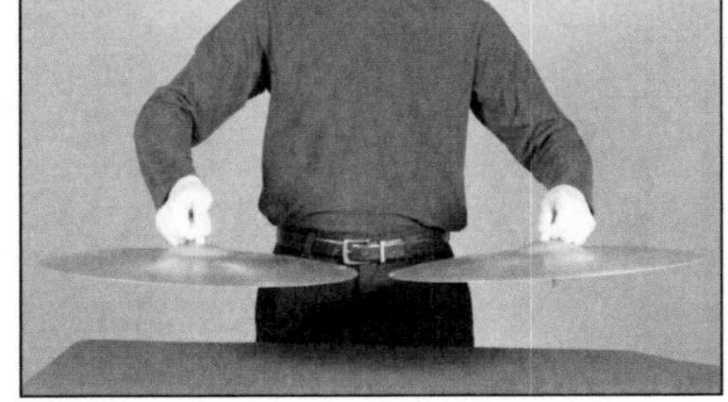

B.

10. Stop the vibration of the cymbals by pressing them firmly into the performer's upper abdominal region.

11. After a crash cymbal passage, always return the cymbals to a padded table as in Step 1.

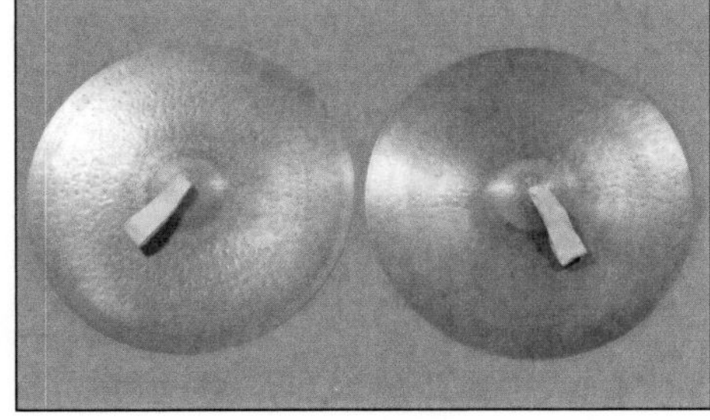

THE SOFT CYMBAL CRASH

Step-By-Step

1. The player must have a padded table large enough to hold two crash cymbals side by side.

2. Place two crash cymbals side by side on a padded table with the straps facing the performer.

3. Imagine holding a pair of snare drum sticks using matched grip. Grasp the cymbal straps as if picking up snare drum sticks with the fulcrum near the bell of the cymbal.

4. Raise both cymbals and hold them perpendicular to the table. Place the bottom edges together on the table.

5. Slowly and quietly close the cymbals and lift them to chest level.

6. Separate the bottom edges while leaving the top edges together. Then, move the bottom edges together to produce a crash. As the crash occurs, separate the cymbals and allow them to vibrate.

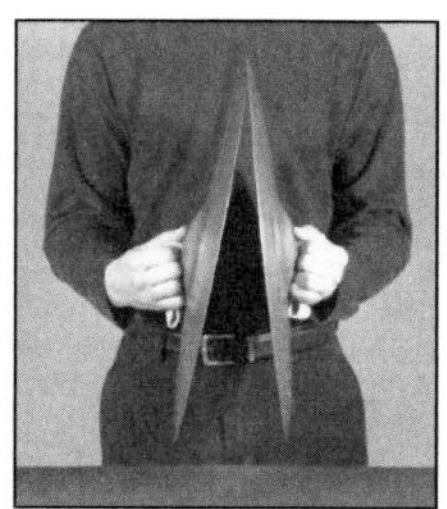

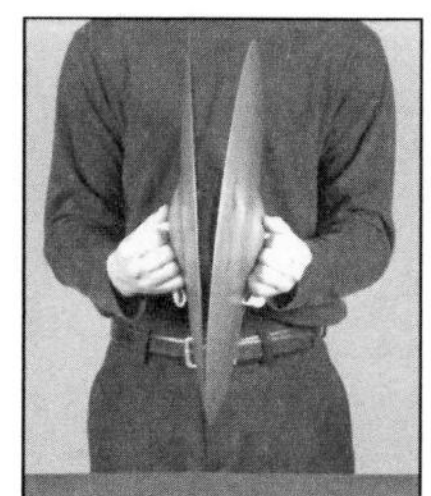

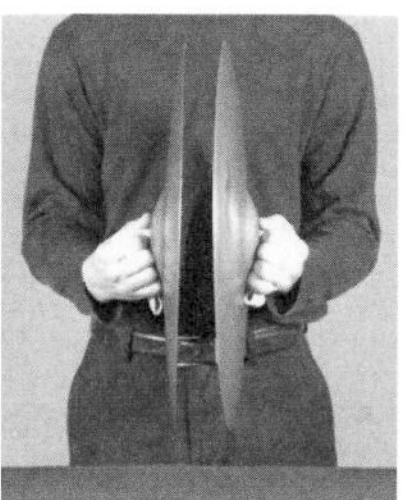

OTHER ISSUES

Dampening the Cymbals

After a crash, pull the edges of the cymbals firmly into the upper abdominal region. Or, place them quietly on a padded table.

Care and Maintenance of Cymbals

Cymbals should be stored flat on a padded shelf in a locked cabinet.

Cleaning concert cymbals is not usually necessary. However, soap and water or a non-abrasive cleanser may be used occasionally to remove an excess build-up of dirt. Avoid buffing.

Tying a Cymbal Knot

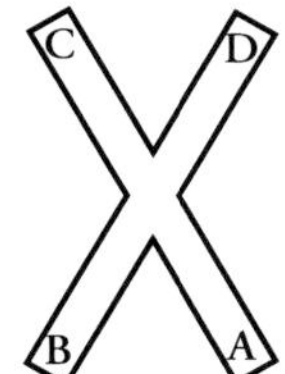

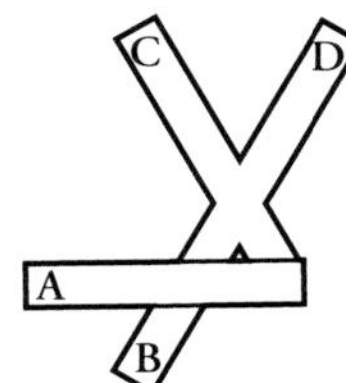

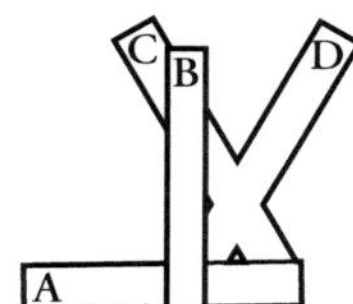

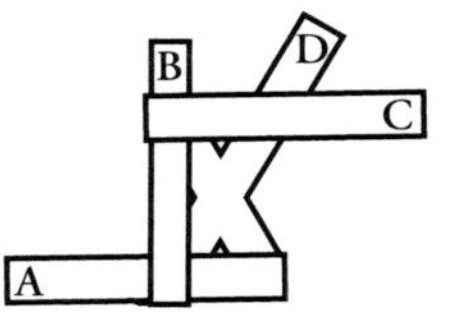

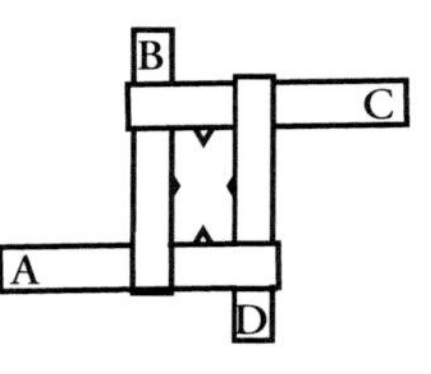

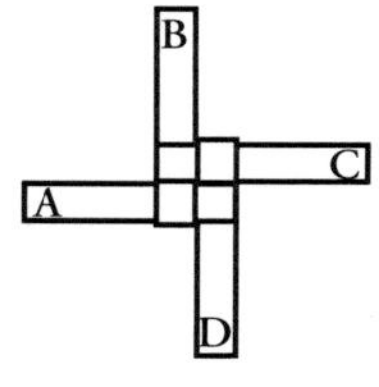

Types of Crash Cymbals

There is a wide variety of weights and sizes of cymbals available. Sizes of cymbals range from 16" to 20". In general, there are four main categories, by weight, of cymbals:

1. Paper thin
2. Thin (French)
3. Medium (Viennese)
4. Thick (German)

Within these categories, cymbals might include additional descriptors, such as "Symphonic" or "Field."

Recommended Cymbals for School Use

- 1 pair of 18" Symphonic Viennese – Recommended for general purpose concert playing
- 1 pair of 16" Symphonic French or Viennese – Recommended for younger (middle school) players because of smaller size and lighter weight

Other Materials Needed

- 1 padded table large enough to hold two large cymbals lying side by side
- Leather cymbal straps, attached using a cymbal knot, not a ball (see "Tying a Cymbal Knot" on previous page)

MINIMUM CRASH CYMBAL SKILLS FOR HIGH SCHOOL GRADUATES

		Student Names			
Skill 1.	Perform staccato ***mf*** quarter note crashes at quarter note = 92 for eight beats.				
Skill 2.	Perform eight ***pp*** whole note crashes at quarter note = 88.				
Skill 3.	Perform ***mp*** sixteenth notes at quarter note = 80 for four beats.				
Skill 4.	Perform a ***ff*** crash. Let ring for four beats at quarter note = 100, then dampen.				
Skill 5.	Perform crash cymbal etude on following page.				

Skill #1
Perform staccato ***mf*** quarter note crashes at quarter note = 92 for eight beats.

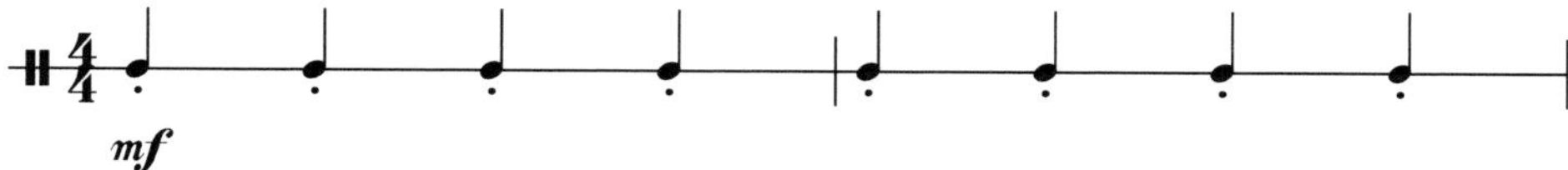

Skill #2
Perform eight ***pp*** whole not crashes at quarter note = 88.

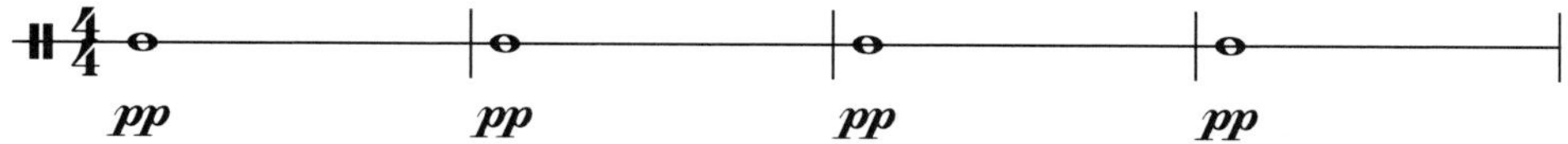

Skill #3
Perform ***mp*** sixteenth notes at quarter note = 80 for four beats.

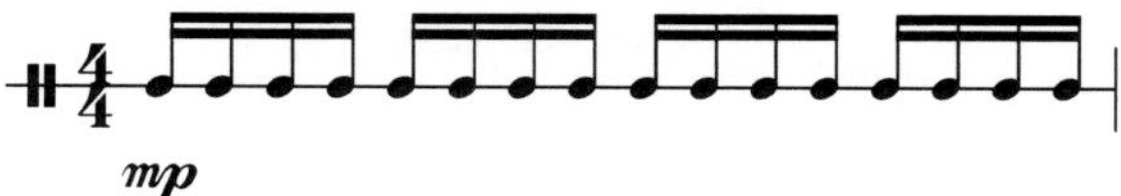

Skill #4
Perform a ***ff*** crash. Let ring for four beats at quarter note = 100, then dampen.

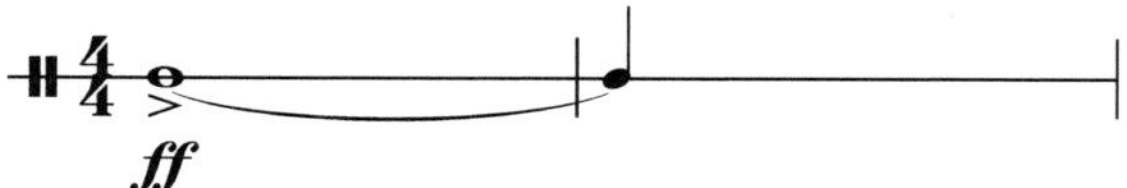

Skill #5
Perform etude below.

Crash Cymbals Etude

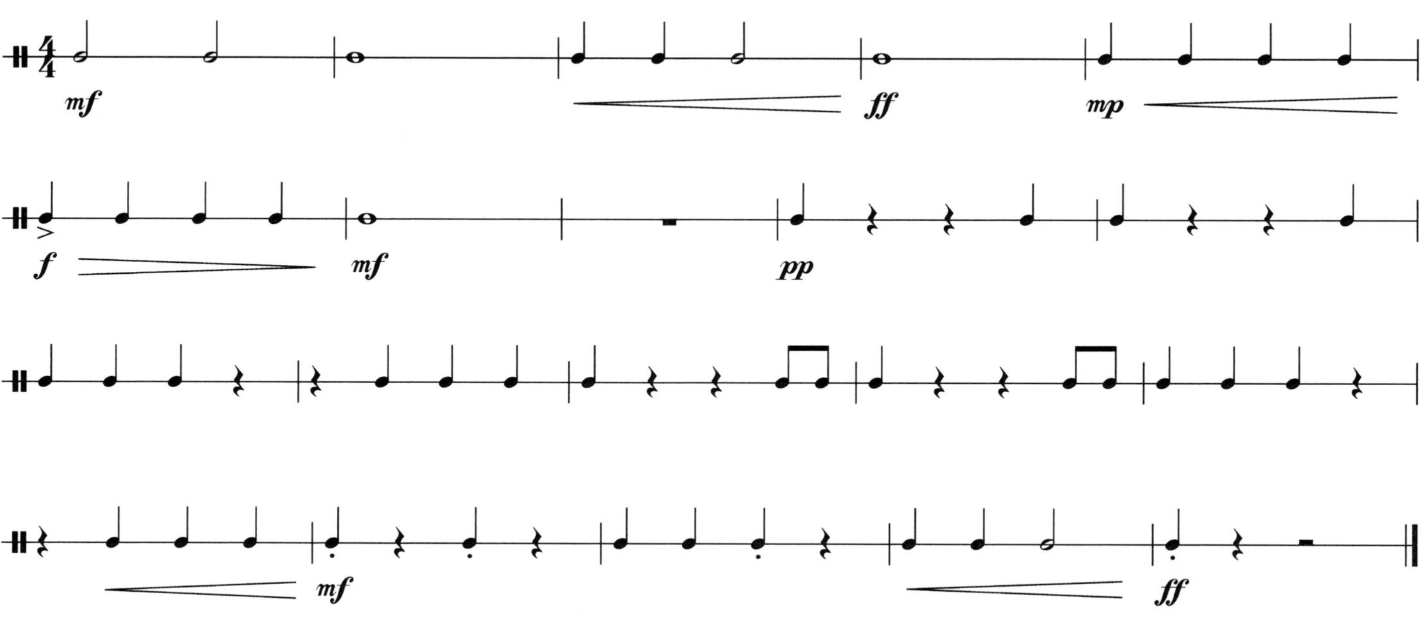

SUSPENDED CYMBAL

The Common Elements

Posture
Grip
Striking Motion
Volume
Sticking
Rolls

POSTURE

Step-By-Step

Height

1. Stand straight with feet slightly apart with weight evenly balanced and arms straight down at sides.

2. Bend arms at the elbows until forearms are parallel to the floor with palms facing the floor.

3. Drop arms from elbow 2-3".

4. Relax wrists and allow fingers to point toward the floor.

5. Height of the suspended cymbal should be adjusted to touch the fingertips as they are in Step 4.

1

2

3

4

5

POSTURE (cont.)

Distance

6. Stand 3 to 4 feet away from the cymbal with mallets in hands and arms in proper playing position.

7. Walk up to the cymbal, stopping when the mallets are over the proper playing area (see below).

Playing Area

For general purpose playing, place one mallet each at three o'clock and nine o'clock on top of the suspended cymbal, about two inches from the edge.

Top View

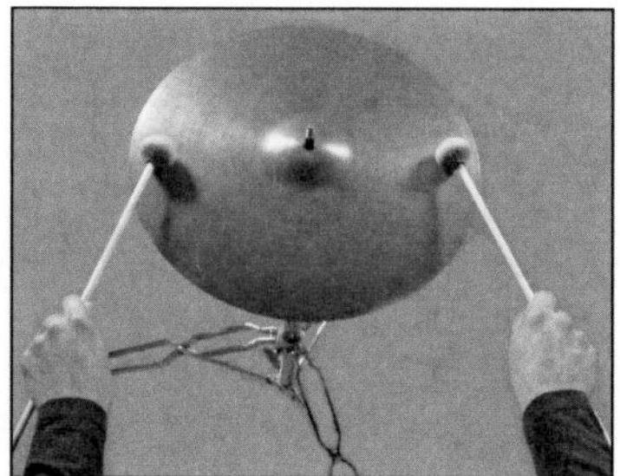

GRIP

Matched grip is used for suspended cymbal playing.

STRIKING MOTION

Piston Motion (see Chapter 1) is applicable to suspended cymbal.

VOLUME

Three factors determine volume when playing a suspended cymbal:

1. Height of mallet/stick from the suspended cymbal.

2. Speed at which the mallet/stick travels toward the cymbal.

3. Type of mallet/stick used

    - Harder mallets/sticks produce greater volume.
    - Softer mallets produce less volume.

STICKING

Sticking on suspended cymbal is usually simple and involves one of the following variations:

1. Single alternating motion (RLRL) – Used to play a roll or more complex rhythms with sticks or mallets.

2. Single hand motion (RRRR or LLLL) – Used to play simple rhythms with a stick on the cymbal.

ROLLS

Notation:  

The roll on suspended cymbal is a single-stroke roll. Mallets or sticks should be positioned at three o'clock and nine o'clock on the cymbal (see "Playing Area" under "Posture" on p. 110).

Roll speed on a suspended cymbal is determined by the desired volume:

Loud Volume = Faster Roll
Soft Volume = Slower Roll

OTHER ISSUES

Dampening

Dampening refers to the method of stopping the vibration (sound) of a suspended cymbal. A suspended cymbal may be dampened by firmly grasping the cymbal at the four o'clock and eight o'clock positions.

Sizes and Types of Suspended Cymbals

Suspended cymbals are available in many different weights, colors, and sizes depending upon their intended function. Types of cymbals are identified by a variety of names, reflecting the various musical settings in which they are used (orchestra, concert band, chamber, jazz, rock, etc.).

For general purpose band or orchestra playing, a 16" or 18" thin or medium thin suspended cymbal is recommended.

Suspended Cymbal Mallets

Most concert suspended cymbal parts can be played using medium soft yarn mallets. Some parts specify the use of a drum stick, in which case any general concert snare drum stick may be used.

Suspended Cymbal Stands

There are two basic types of suspended cymbal stands: "goose neck" and "traditional." The goose neck stand is used to suspend one crash cymbal by its strap and is seldom used. The traditional stand is used to support a suspended cymbal (see photo below).

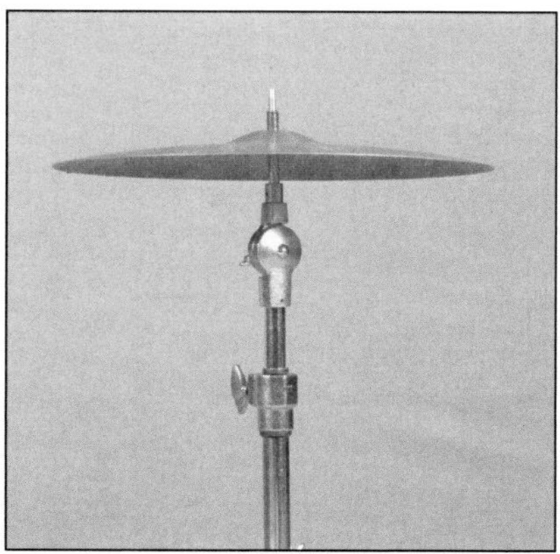

Recommended Characteristics of a Suspended Cymbal for School Use

Size:	16" to 18" for general purpose playing
Thickness:	Thin or Medium Thin

Other Equipment Needed

1. Suspended cymbal stand
   - Height adjustable
   - Free of rattles

2. Cymbal sleeve (traditional stand only)
   - Rubber or plastic

3. Cymbal felt (traditional stand only)
   - One felt disc 1/2" to 1" thick to place on stand between stand and bell of cymbal

4. Mallets
   - Medium soft yarn for rolls and single long notes
   - Snare drum sticks for fast articulate passages, short chokes, and loud, articulate notes

MINIMUM SUSPENDED CYMBAL SKILLS FOR HIGH SCHOOL GRADUATES

		Student Names			
Skill 1.	Demonstrate a roll at quarter note = 100 starting at *pp* and ending *ff* using appropriate roll speed.				
Skill 2.	Perform *mf* sixteenth notes at quarter note = 80 using snare drum sticks.				
Skill 3.	Perform a roll at quarter note = 120 starting *pp* and ending *f*. Dampen immediately.				
Skill 4.	Perform staccato *f* quarter note chokes at quarter note = 92.				

Skill #1
Demonstrate a roll at quarter note = 100 starting at *pp* and ending *ff* using appropriate roll speed.

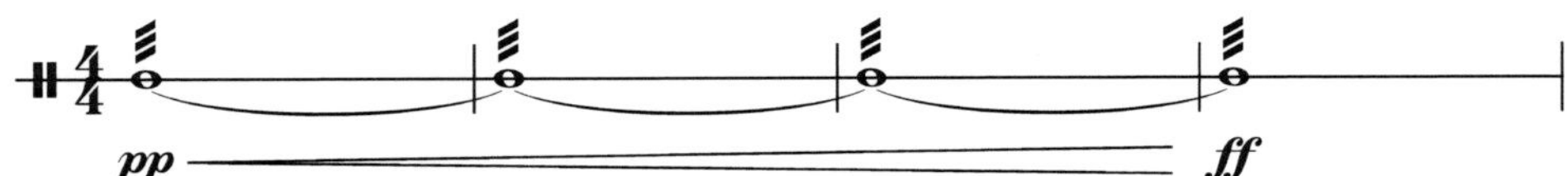

Skill #2
Perform *mf* sixteenth notes at quarter note = 80 using snare drumsticks.

Skill #3
Perform a roll at quarter note = 120 starting *pp* and ending *f*. Dampen immediately.

Skill #4
Perform staccato *f* quarter note chokes at quarter note = 92.

TRIANGLE

Posture
Grip
Striking Motion
Volume
Sticking
Rolls

POSTURE

Step-By-Step

1. Stand straight with hands relaxed and to the sides of the body.
2. Raise left hand, bending the elbow until the forearm is parallel to the floor.
3. Turn the hand until the thumb is facing the ceiling. Form a "C" with the fingers and thumb
4. With the right hand, rest the triangle clip on the thumb and index finger.
5. Place the triangle on the tringle clip. The triangle should hang freely without touching any part of the hand. Raise the triangle to eye level.

1

2

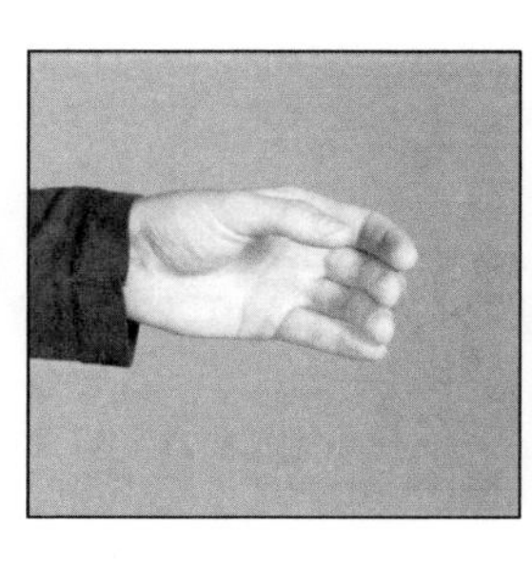
3

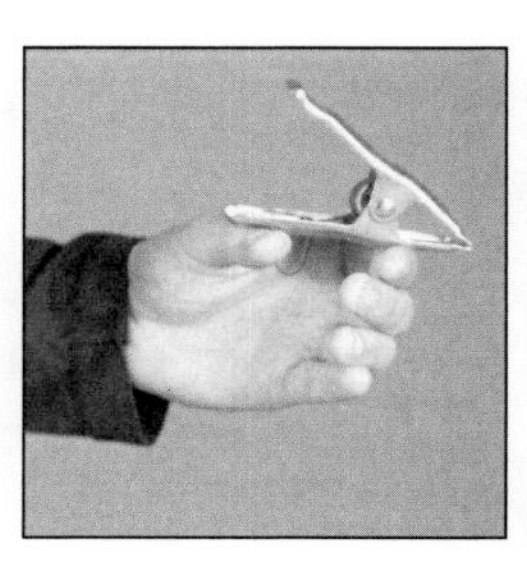
4

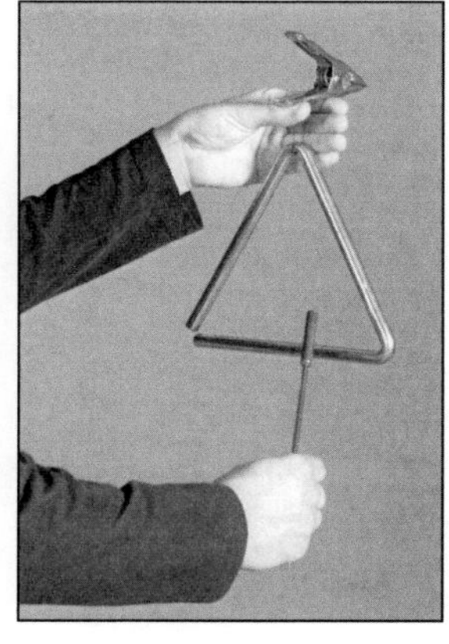
5

POSTURE (cont.)

Playing Area

The triangle should be struck at the point along the bottom edge that produces the most characteristic sound – an indefinitely pitched "shimmer." The exact spot may vary from instrument to instrument.

GRIP

Matched grip is used to hold the triangle beater.

STRIKING MOTION

The piston motion discussed in Chapter 1 is the primary means of striking a triangle. The triangle is struck with the beater at a slight angle to the base of the triangle.

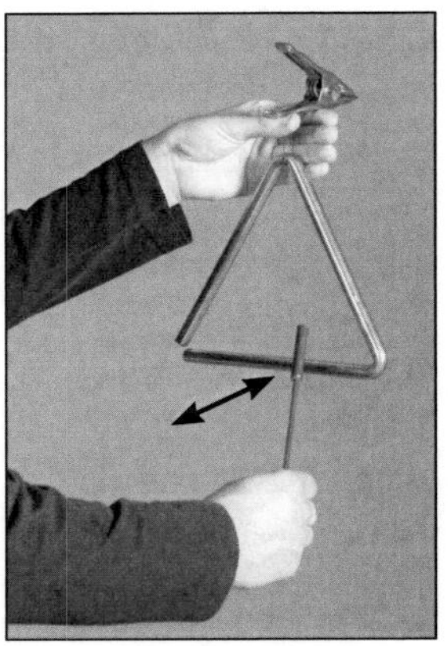

VOLUME

Three primary factors determine volume when playing a triangle:

1. **Distance (height) of the Beater from the Triangle**
   Less Distance = Less Volume
   Greater Distance = More Volume

2. **Size (thickness) of the Beater**
   Thin Beater = Less Volume
   Thicker Beater = More Volume

3. **Size of the Triangle**
   Small Triangle = Less Volume
   Larger Triangle = More Volume

STICKING

The triangle is normally played with one beater. However, for passages that are too fast to execute with one hand, the triangle may be suspended from a music stand and struck with a pair of matched beaters.

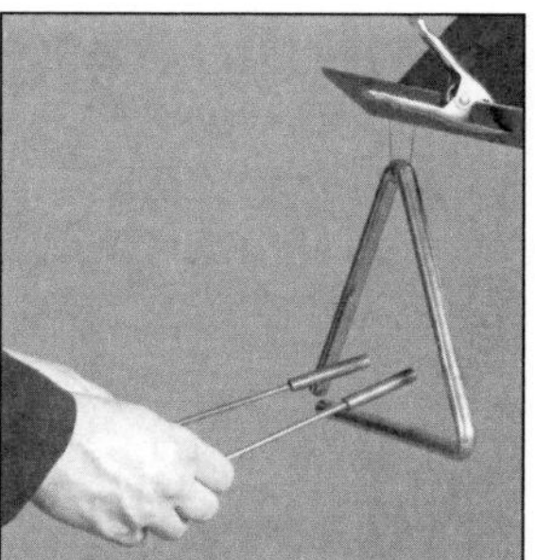

ROLLS

Rolls are executed between the lower edge of the triangle and the adjacent closed angle.

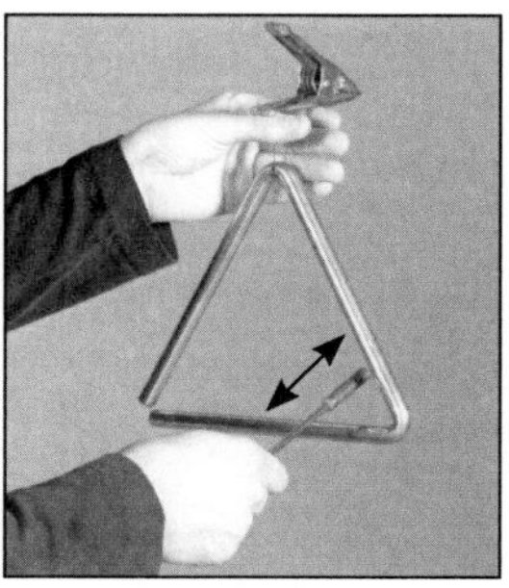

OTHER ISSUES

Muffling

While holding the triangle with the left hand, leave the thumb and index finger in place and close the remaining fingers firmly around the triangle. The instrument should be muffled after it has been struck, not while striking, unless otherwise specified in the music.

Sizes of Triangles

Triangles come in many sizes, from approximately 4" to 10". General purpose triangles range from 6" to 9".

Triangle Beaters

For general purpose playing, one should have access to matched pairs of small, medium, and large triangle beaters.

OTHER ISSUES (cont.)

Triangle Clip

The triangle clip or holder may be made of a variety of materials, such as a large wooden clothespin or a metal clamp (available at most hardware stores). Holders are also manufactured by percussion companies. A holder should have two holes drilled approximately 1" apart in the middle of one side of the clip. Using light weight string, such as 20 lb. braided casting line, tie a loop between the holes just long enough so the triangle does not touch the clip (no longer than 1/2"). Tie a second "safety" loop approximately the same length.

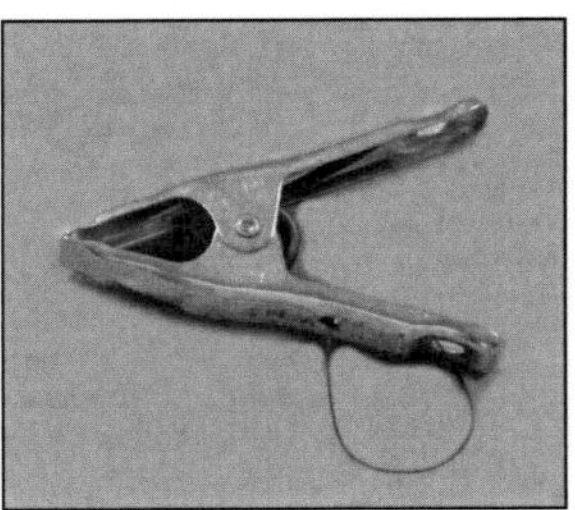

Recommended Characteristics of a Triangle for School Use
6" to 9"
Long decay
High, shimmering overtones
No definite pitch

Other Materials Needed
Clip with light-weight string (see above)
Padded table or stand.
In a rehearsal situation, the triangle and beaters should be laid flat on a padded surface when not being played.

MINIMUM TRIANGLE SKILLS FOR HIGH SCHOOL GRADUATES

		Student Names			
Skill 1.	Demonstrate a roll at quarter note = 100 starting ***pp*** and ending ***ff*** using appropriate roll speed.				
Skill 2.	Perform ***mf*** sixteenth notes at quarter note = 92 using two beaters.				
Skill 3.	Perform a a four-beat roll at quarter note = 120 starting ***p*** and ending ***f***. Dampen immediately.				
Skill 4.	Perform ***pp*** staccato eighth notes at quarter = 80. Dampen between notes.				
Skill 5.	Perform triangle etude on next page.				

MINIMUM TRIANGLE SKILLS FOR HIGH SCHOOL GRADUATES (cont.)

Skill #1

Demonstrate a roll at quarter note = 100 starting *pp* and ending *ff* using appropriate roll speed.

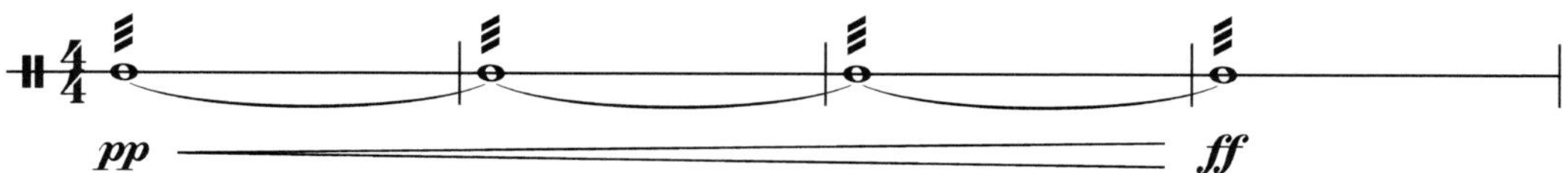

Skill #2

Perform *mf* sixteenth notes at quarter note = 92 using two beaters.

Skill #3

Perform a four-beat roll at quarter note = 120 starting *p* and ending *f*. Dampen immediately.

Skill #4

Perform *pp* staccato eighth notes at quarter = 80. Dampen between notes.

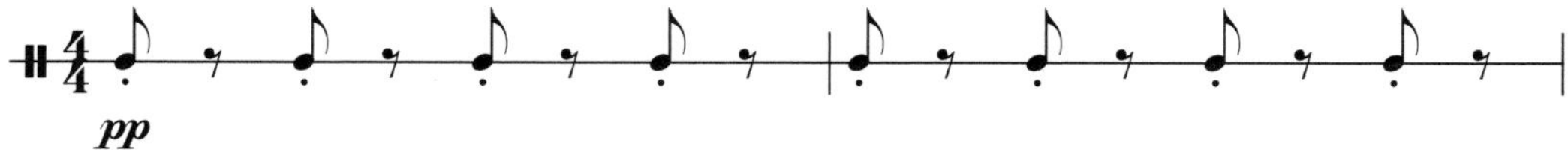

Skill #5

Perform the following triangle etude.

Triangle Etude

TAMBOURINE

The Common Elements

Posture
Grip
Striking Motion
Volume
Sticking
Rolls

POSTURE

Stand straight with feet apart, weight evenly balanced.

GRIP

Step-By-Step

1. With the hand that will hold the tambourine, grip an imaginary snare drum stick using matched grip.

2. Maintaining correct matched grip, turn the hand over so the palm side of the hand faces the ceiling.

3. With the tambourine head facing the ceiling, insert the shell of the tambourine into the hand so the tambourine is supported firmly by the fingers and palm.

4. The thumb may be placed on the side of the shell or on the tambourine head for added stability.

5. Hold the tambourine approximately at a 45-degree angle.

STRIKING MOTION

The tambourine is held in one hand while the other hand uses Piston Motion to strike the instrument.

VOLUME

Volume is determined by two factors:

1. Distance between the tambourine head and the striking hand.

2. How and where the tambourine is struck:
    - **Soft** – Heel of hand rests in the center of head and tambourine is struck on the rim using fingertips.
    - **Medium/General Purpose** – Thumb and fingertips or knuckles strike the tambourine head off-center
    - **Loud** – Tambourine is struck in center of head using the fist (palm down)

STICKING

1. **General Purpose Playing**
    - The tambourine is held with one hand and struck with the other.

2. **Soft/Medium Rapidly-Moving Passages**
    - Place tambourine on a padded table or stand, head facing ceiling or balance tambourine on knee.
    - Play passage using fingertips on rim, off-center.

3. **Loud, Rapidly-Moving Passages**
    - Hold the tambourine with head facing the floor.
    - Hold one knee up by placing a foot on a chair or bench.
    - Alternately strike tambourine in center of head using the fist of the striking hand and the knee.

ROLLS

There are two types of rolls used in tambourine performance: the shake roll and the thumb (or finger) roll. The type of roll used depends upon two factors:

Volume:	Soft	Thumb/Finger Roll
	Loud	Shake Roll
Duration:	Shorter	Thumb/Finger Roll
	Longer	Shake Roll

ROLLS (cont.)

THE THUMB/FINGER ROLL

Step-By-Step

1. Hold the tambourine with one hand at a slight angle to the floor, head facing the ceiling.

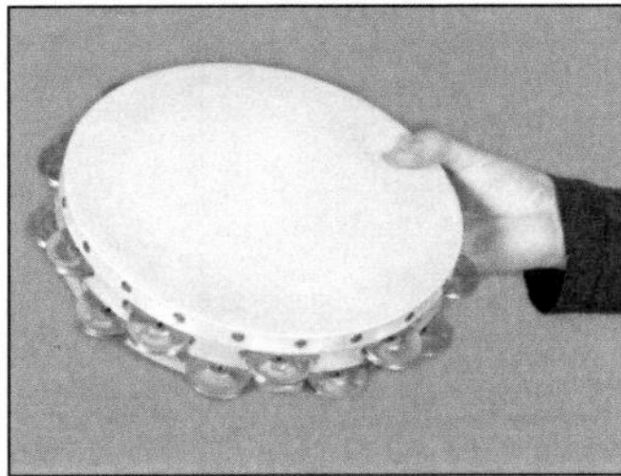

2. With the other hand, place the thumb as illustrated below.

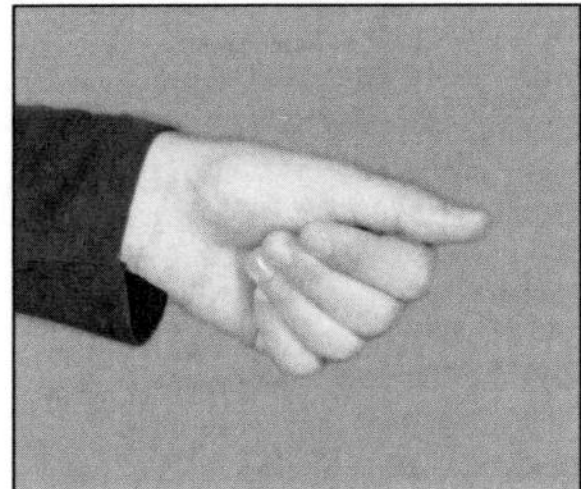

3. Maintaining the hand position illustrated above, rotate the wrist so that the tip of the thumb can be placed on top off the tambourine head.

4. Apply just enough pressure to the thumb to create friction between the thumb and the head.

5. Keeping the thumb as close to the edge of the tambourine as possible and maintaining the right amount of pressure, trace the rim of the tambourine with the tip of the thumb.

NOTE
Most difficulties occur when too much pressure is applied. Some experimentation may be necessary to determine the "right" amount of pressure. Some players find it helpful to apply a thin coat of beeswax around the edge of the tambourine head.

THE SHAKE ROLL

Step-By-Step

1. Hold the tambourine at the performer's side, with the tambourine head facing the body.

2. Raise the tambourine so that it is at ear level, slightly in front of the body, with the head facing the player's ear.

3. Strike the tambourine with the other hand, then immediately rotate the wrist in a back-and-forth circular motion, as if screwing in a light bulb.

4. Strike the tambourine to end the roll, simultaneously returning it to a horizontal position.

Tambourine Roll Exercise

Recommended Characteristics of a Tambourine for School Use

Diameter:	10 inches
Jingles:	Double row
Shell:	Wooden
Head:	Calfskin or pre-tuned

MINIMUM TAMBOURINE SKILLS FOR HIGH SCHOOL GRADUATES

		Student Names			
Skill 1.	Perform a four-beat shake roll starting a ***mp*** and ending ***ff*** at quarter note = 100.				
Skill 2.	Demonstrate ***f*** sixteenth notes using the knee-fist technique for four beats at quarter note = 120.				
Skill 3.	Perform ***mp*** sixteenth notes for four beats at quarter note = 88.				
Skill 4.	Perform ***mf*** quarter note thumb rolls at quarter note = 88.				
Skill 5.	Perform tambourine etude on next page.				

MINIMUM TAMBOURINE SKILLS FOR HIGH SCHOOL GRADUATES (cont.)

Skill #1

Perform a four-beat shake roll starting a ***mp*** and ending ***ff*** at quarter note = 100.

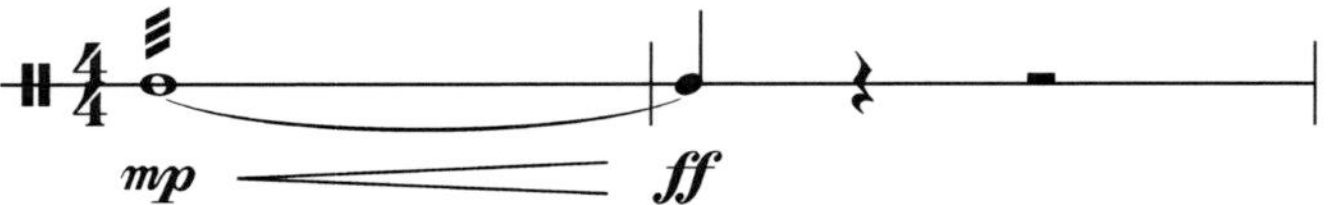

Skill #2

Demonstrate ***f*** sixteenth notes using the knee-fist technique for four beats at quarter note = 120.

Skill #3

Perform ***mp*** sixteenth notes for four beats at quarter note = 88.

Skill #4

Perform ***mf*** quarter note thumb rolls at quarter note = 88.

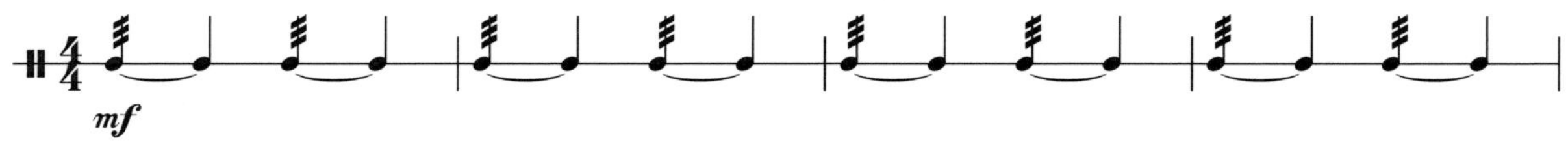

Skill #5

Perform the following tambourine etude.

Tambourine Etude

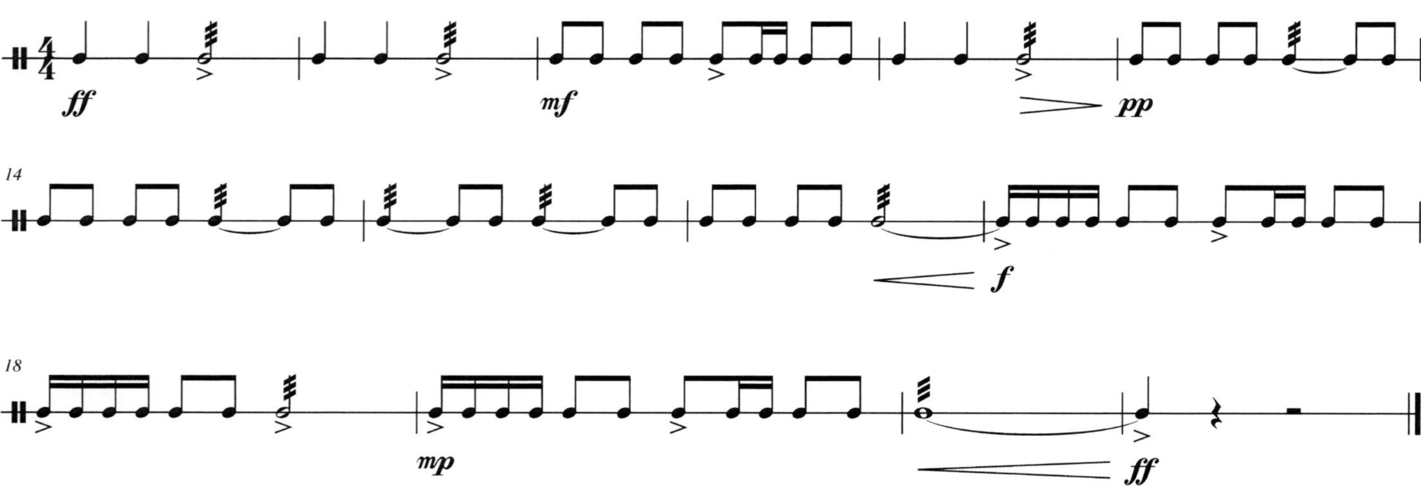

Chapter 7

DRUM SET

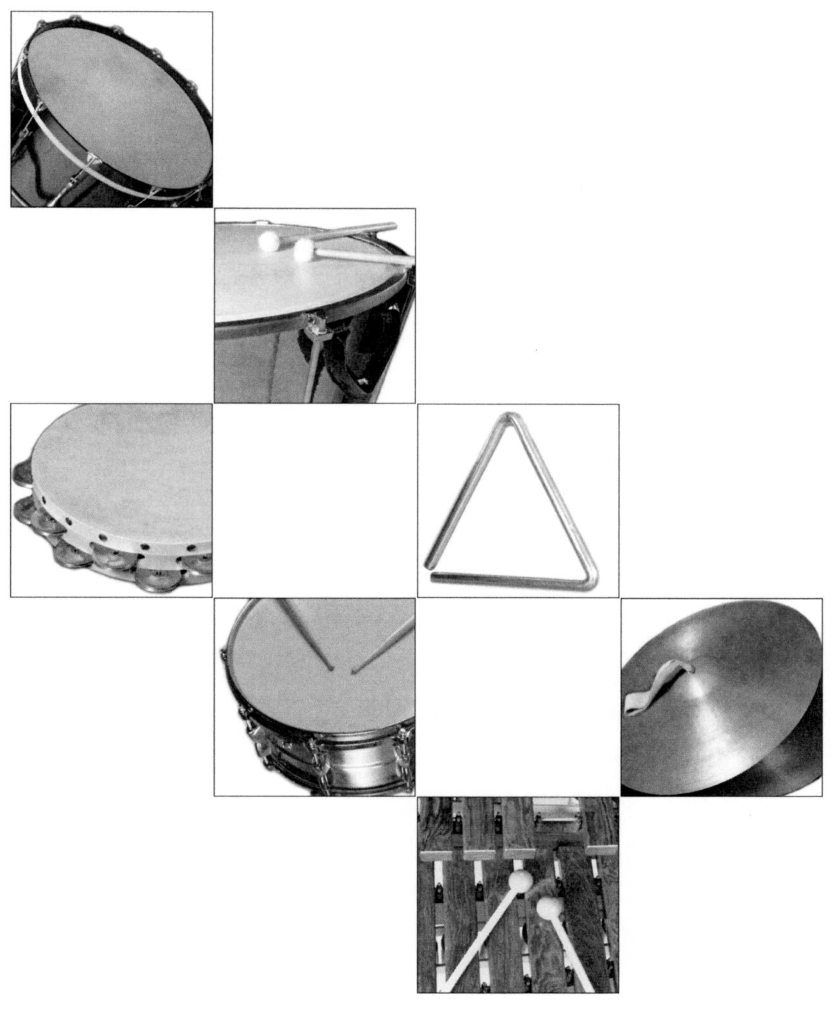

Chapter 7

DRUM SET

The Common Elements

Posture
Grip
Striking Motion
Volume
Sticking
Rolls

Many young people have visions of being a famous drum set player. Their visions, as well as their parents' visions, may overshadow the practical implications of playing drum set. Like any artistic journey, success depends upon dedication, hard work, and persistence. In an effort to have the best experience, consider the following essential components to ultimate success.

Every aspiring drum set player should:

1. Study with a competent, well-rounded teacher.
2. Learn through a sequential curriculum.
3. Study various styles of music, listen to recordings, and constantly observe great players.

Getting the Right Start

Success is more likely when the aspiring player studies from an experienced teacher. While affirmative answers to the following questions cannot ensure quality education, a "yes" answer can increase the probability that private lessons will be more beneficial to students.

Questions to ask when searching for a private teacher:

1. Do you have a degree in music?
2. Do you require students to use a specific counting system?
3. Do you require students to use matched grip?
4. Do you require students to read music?
5. Do you require students to learn other percussion instruments such as marimba and timpani?

Investing in a Drum Set

There are many excellent brands of drum sets on the market. When purchasing a drum set, always invest in high quality cymbals (Zildjian, Paiste, Sabian). Inexpensive, poor quality cymbals will render an otherwise high quality drum set ineffective. The student will need a pair of hi-hat cymbals (14"), a basic ride cymbal (18-20") and a crash cymbal (16"). High achievers will soon need one additional ride cymbal and one or two additional crash cymbals of varying sizes. Start with a basic five-piece drum set (bass drum, snare drum, two mounted tom-toms, and a floor tom) with high quality cymbals. Many professional drummers use a basic five-piece drum set for the duration of their career.

MINIMUM DRUM SET SKILLS FOR HIGH SCHOOL GRADUATES

	Student Names			
1. Demonstrate correct posture.				
2. Demonstrate the application of each basic style on page 140.				
3. Demonstrate effective reading skills.				

POSTURE

Refer to Chapter 1, page 4 for detailed information about posture.

When determining correct posture, consider the following items in order.

1. Baseline
2. Playing Area
3. Height of Drum Throne/Height of Drums and Cymbals
4. Distance (of instruments from body)

POSTURE (cont.)

BASELINE

Baseline refers to relaxed, natural position of the body. Determine the baseline position by simply walking in a free, unencumbered manner, as if going for a stroll in the park. Always establish the body's natural baseline posture before playing an instrument. Keep the head up and maintain the body's natural position when sitting at the drum set.

PLAYING AREA

Playing area refers to the area on any percussion instruments that, when struck, produces the most characteristic (resonant) sound. For example, a snare drum and tom-tom should be played slightly off center. Suspended cymbals most often will be struck halfway between the edge and center, but this will vary, depending on the desired sound.

HEIGHT OF THE DRUM THRONE

Step-By-Step

1. While standing, adjust height of drum throne so that when sitting, there is a slight downward slope from the hips to the knees.
2. Stand straight with arms relaxed at sides.
3. Sit on the correctly adjusted drum throne. Feet should extend two-to-three inches in front of the knees in a relaxed, natural manner.
4. Rest hands on lap in a relaxed, natural manner.

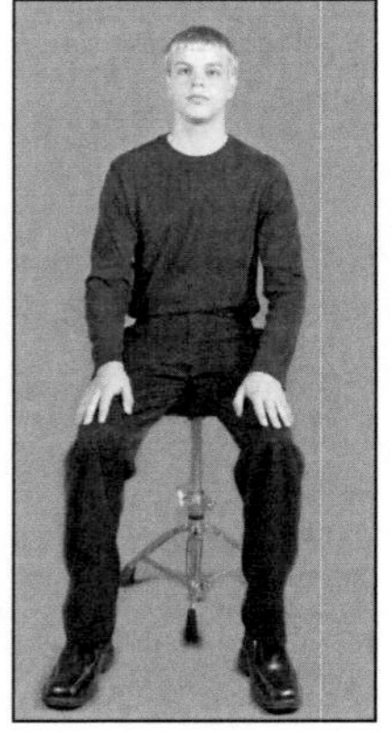

HEIGHT OF THE SNARE DRUM AND HI-HAT

Once the player is sitting correctly on the drum throne and the snare drum is in place, adjust the height of the drum. While sitting, apply the same information as presented on page 30 of Chapter 3. Following this procedure will allow the player to sit correctly and play drums in the correct playing areas without having to lean into or away from the instruments. Apply the same process to the floor tom.

The hi-hat should be slightly higher than the snare drum. The player's arms should remain at the same level as playing the snare drum and floor tom.

HEIGHT OF THE RIDE CYMBAL

The ride cymbal should be slightly higher than the floor tom at a gradual angle toward the player. The player's arm should remain at the same level as playing the snare drum, floor tom, and hi-hat.

DISTANCE OF INSTRUMENTS FROM THE BODY

Distance refers to the space between the body and the instrument. In general, correct distance from the instrument is determined by following the procedure below.

Bass Drum (Pedal)

While sitting on a correctly adjusted drum throne, with feet extended 2 to 3 inches in front of the knees, place the bass drum pedal under the foot (for a right-handed drummer). Do not move the foot forward or backward. Leave it in a natural position.

DISTANCE OF INSTRUMENTS FROM THE BODY (cont.)

Hi-Hat (Pedal)

While sitting on a correctly adjusted drum throne, with the right foot comfortably placed on the bass drum pedal, move the left foot approximately 12 inches to the left foot.

Snare Drum, Tom-Toms, and Ride Cymbal

While sitting on a correctly adjusted drum throne, with the right foot comfortably placed on the bass drum pedal and the left foot placed on the hi-hat pedal, insert the snare drum between the legs and adjust the toms so they can be played in the correct playing area without overly extending the arms. Position the basic ride cymbal on a cymbal stand to the right side of the player as shown in the photo below.

GRIP

Matched grip is recommended for general drum set playing. Refer to page 4 in Chapter 1. Occasionally, drum set players develop a "thumbs up" approach to playing the ride cymbal (usually the right hand for right-handed players). This is similar to the thumbs up grip on timpani (French grip) and is acceptable when monitored by a responsible teacher.

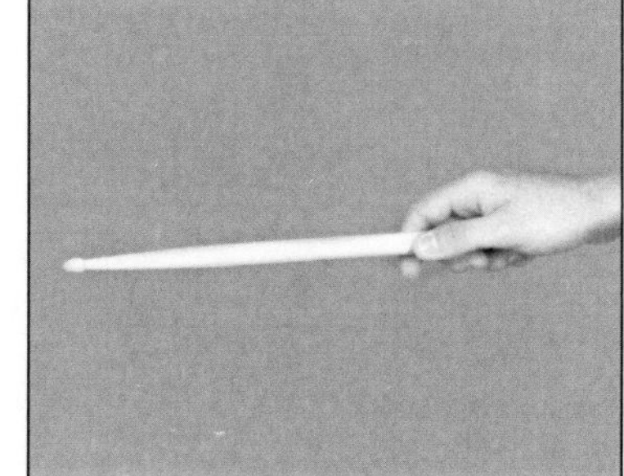

Matched Grip

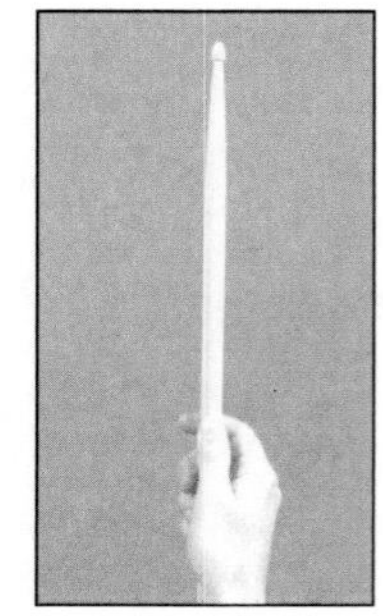

Thumbs Up

STRIKING MOTION

The Piston Motion is recommended. Refer to page 6, Chapter 1.

VOLUME

Refer to page 7, Chapter 1.

STICKING

Refer to pages 8-9, Chapter 1.

ROLLS

Refer to page 11, Chapter 1.

STYLES

Proficient drum set playing is based on two issues: developing independence and applying independent techniques to a variety of music styles. Any aspiring player should listen to and practice a variety of styles, such as swing, rock, Latin, and country. Since independence involves the complex operation of the complete body, introduce one instrument at a time when beginning a new style. Practice each style in several different tempos.

Basic Rock

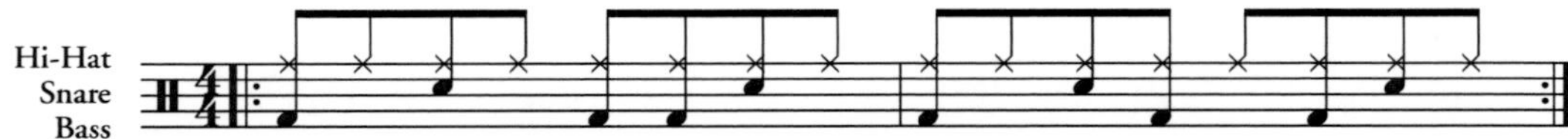

Swing

Samba

Bossa Nova

Jazz Waltz

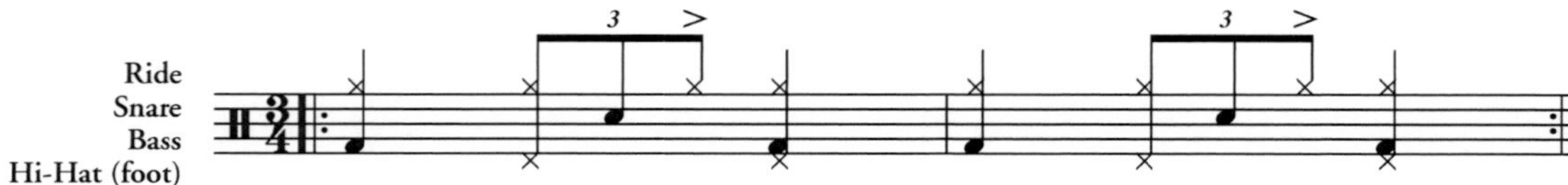

Country Two-Step

SELECT DRUM SET RESOURCES

The following is a list of sources for learning and developing independence and musical styles. Feel free to edit this brief list as needed.

Groove Essentials	Tommy Igoe	Hudson Music
The Jazz Drummer's Reading Workbook	Tom Morgan	C. Alan Publications, LLC
Percussion Techniques (DVD-ROM)	Ron Brough	C. Alan Publications, LLC
Reggae Drumming	Peter Epting	C. Alan Publications, LLC

Chapter 8

HOW TO APPLY COMMON ELEMENTS APPROACH IN A REHEARSAL SITUATION

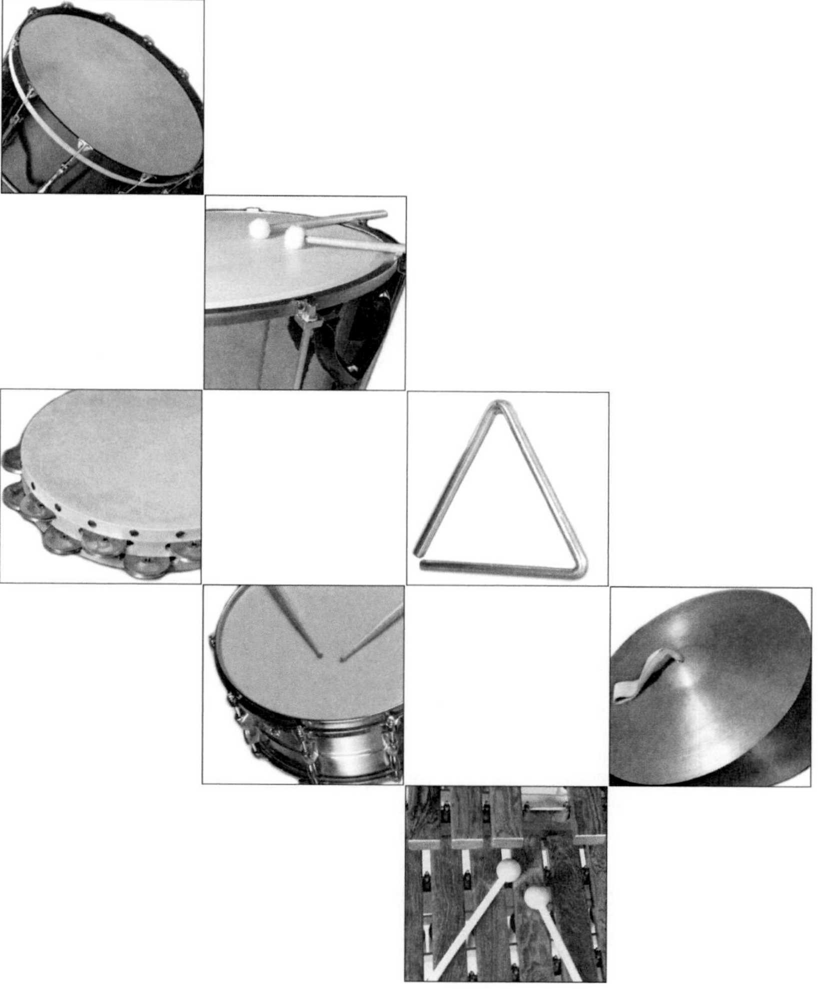

Chapter 8

HOW TO APPLY THE COMMON ELEMENTS APPROACH IN A REHEARSAL SITUATION

Applying the Common Elements in rehearsal situations is an important feature of the success of young percussionists. Whether a conductor is standing on a podium or moving around the room, the process is similar. First, use the visual approach. Frequently LOOK at the percussionists and FIX what you see. Keep in mind that most issues inherent in the Common Element approach can be seen. If a percussionist's physical form is correct, he/she will most likely produce a good sound. Develop a habit of focusing your visual attention on the percussion section several times during a rehearsal.

Limiting your visual search may be helpful. That is, decide in advance which Common Element you will focus on. Keep a check list of the Common Elements and focus on different elements on a rotating basis.

Monday	Posture (Distance)
Tuesday	Posture (Distance)
Wednesday	Striking Motion (Piston Motion)
Thursday	Striking Motion (Piston Motion)
Friday	Posture (Distance)

While you may SEE other issues that may deserve your attention, focus on helping students FIX the issues you have selected for any given rehearsal. Remember that the Common Elements approach is hierarchal. Upper levels depend on the successful attainment of lower levels. Correct use of one element enables a percussionist to move toward the next level in the hierarchy.

BASIC	**Posture:**	The result of good posture is good sound.
↑	**Grip:**	The result of correct grip is good sound.
	Striking Motion:	The result of perfect striking motion is good sound production.
	Volume:	The result of dynamic control is positive musical effect.
↓	**Sticking:**	The result of effective stickings is positive musical effect.
ADVANCED	**Rolls:**	The result of effectively executing rolls is positive musical effect.

LOOK, LISTEN & REPEAT

Take a mental picture of whatever you are searching for – it takes only a glance. Then, REWARD the correct attribute or FIX it if necessary. This is a similar process used by conductors to monitor the development of any musician in an ensemble.

The success of any method or procedure depends on its effective application in a rehearsal situation. It depends on a good teacher. Providing information that will enable musicians to act independently is the ultimate goal of a learning environment. When musicians are empowered to make informed decisions there will be an increased probability of having a superior group.

Step-By-Step

1. Look at the percussion section several times during every rehearsal.
2. Plan in advance the issue that you are seeking to improve.
3. Address the issue and ask students to verbalize "how to fix" the problem.
4. Look again at the percussion section to provide reinforcement.
5. Compliment incremental improvement.
6. At the next rehearsal, revisit the issue and reinforce noticeable improvements.
7. Each percussionist will have different issues to address as development occurs.
8. On a rotating schedule, focus on specific Common Elements each day, each week, and each month throughout the school term.

SOLVING PROBLEMS

On the following pages are the percussion parts to the first movement of ***Homage to Normandy*** (C. Alan Publications © 1997), a composition for band by David J. Long. Examine each part and determine issues that may arise in a typical rehearsal situation. List each issue and provide solutions.

Percussion 1
Bells
Tam-Tam
Chimes

HOMAGE TO NORMANDY

I. Elegy: For All of the Fallen

David J. Long

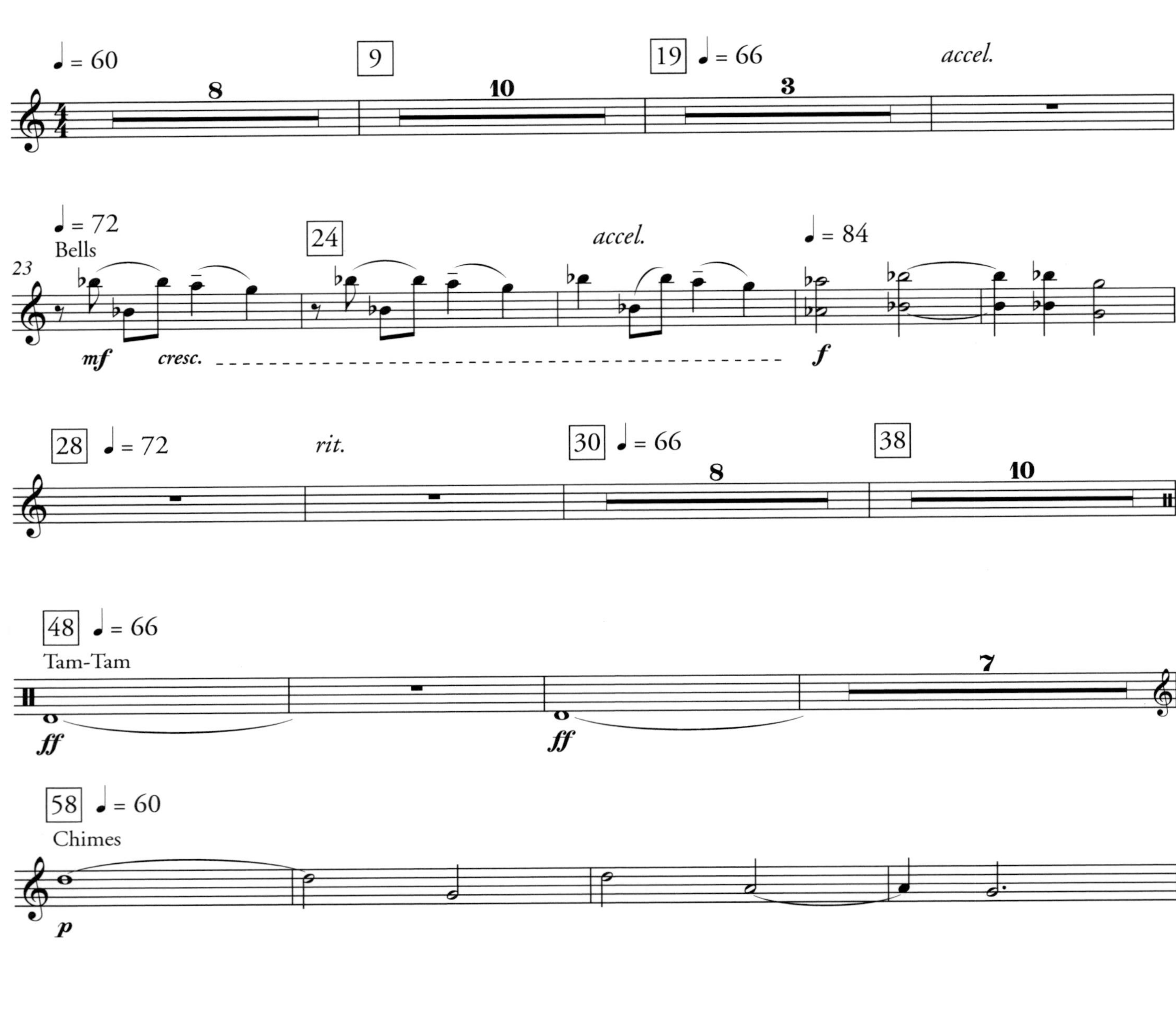

Percussion 2
Snare Drum

HOMAGE TO NORMANDY

I. Elegy: For All of the Fallen

David J. Long

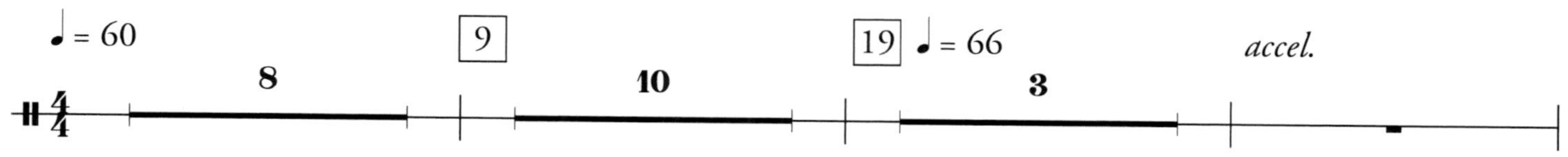

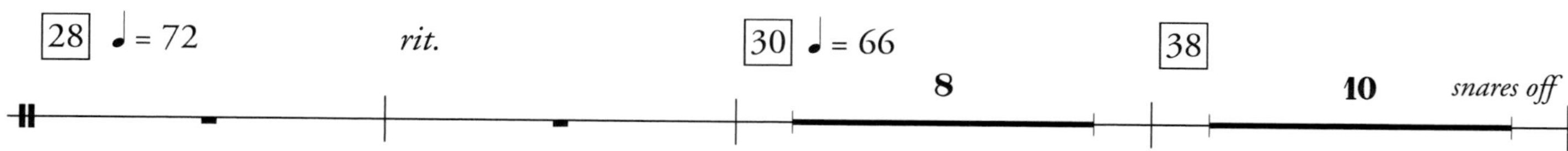

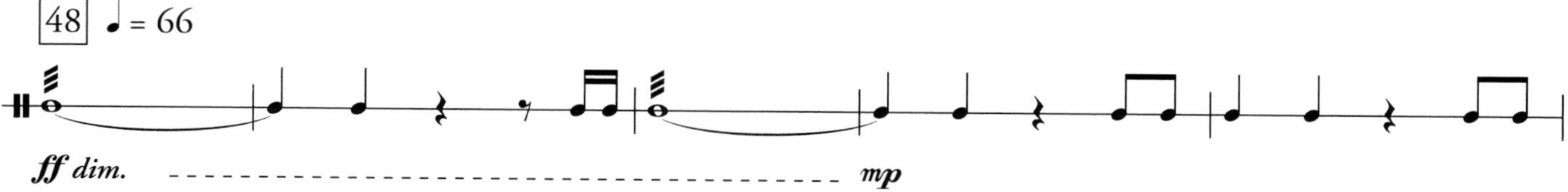

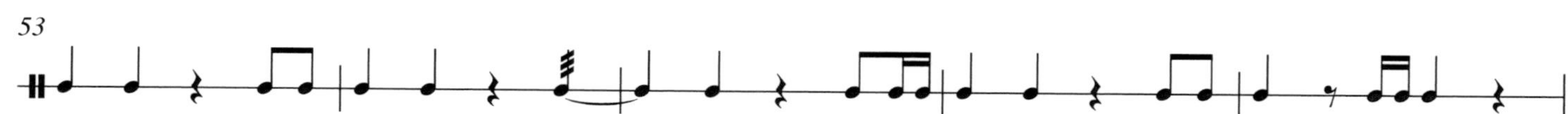

Percussion 3
Suspended Cymbal
Crash Cymbals

HOMAGE TO NORMANDY

I. Elegy: For All of the Fallen

David J. Long

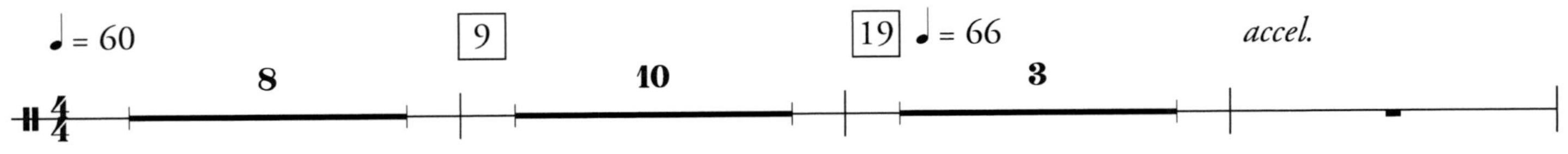

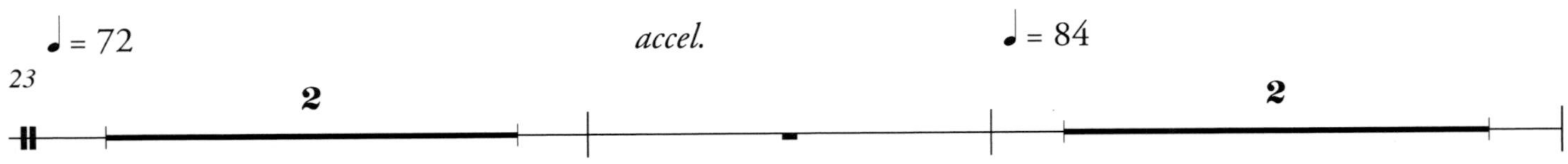

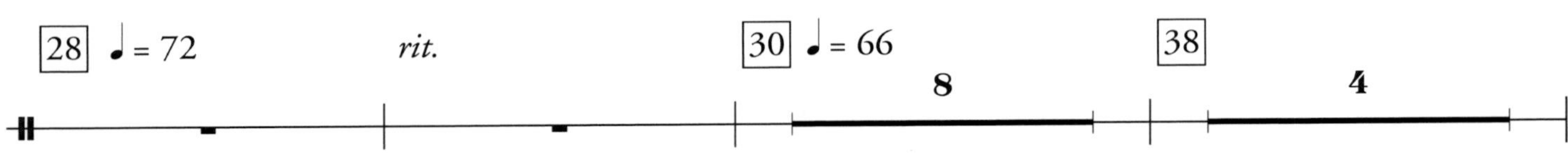

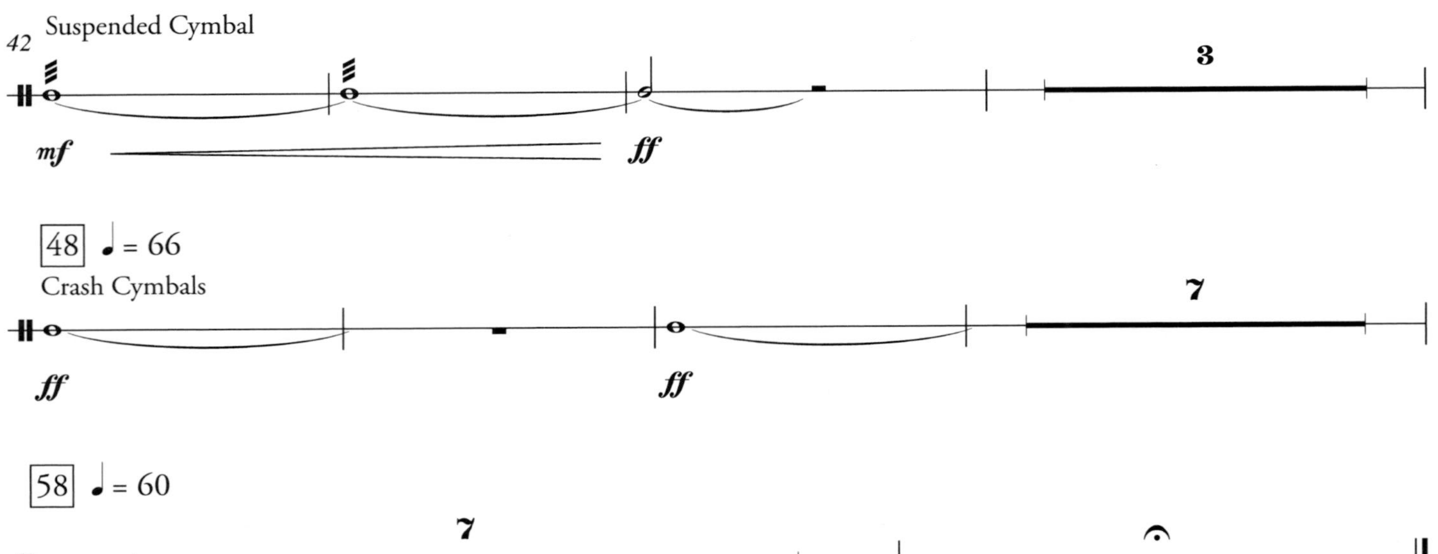

Percussion 4
Bass Drum

HOMAGE TO NORMANDY

I. Elegy: For All of the Fallen

David J. Long

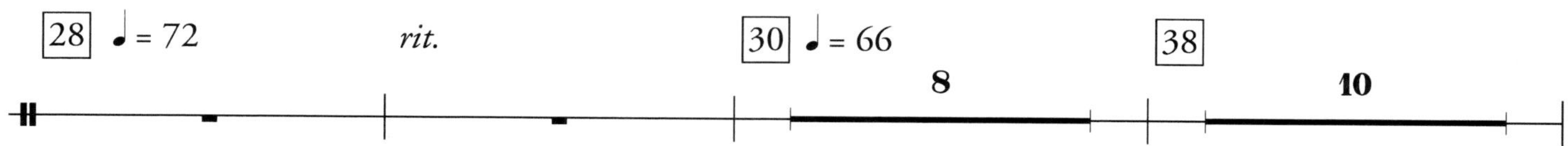

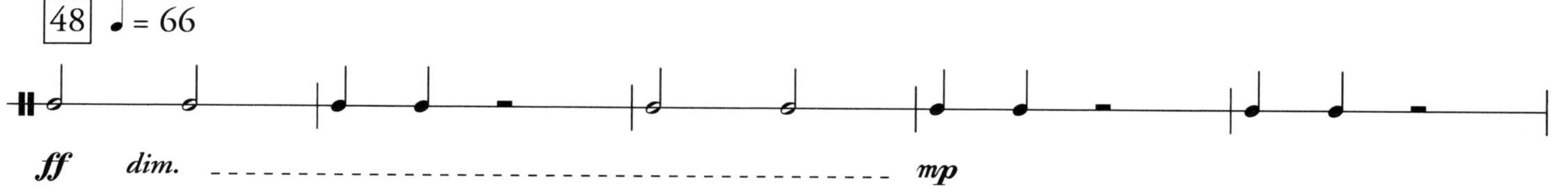

Timpani
(G-D-E♭)

HOMAGE TO NORMANDY

I. Elegy: For All of the Fallen

David J. Long

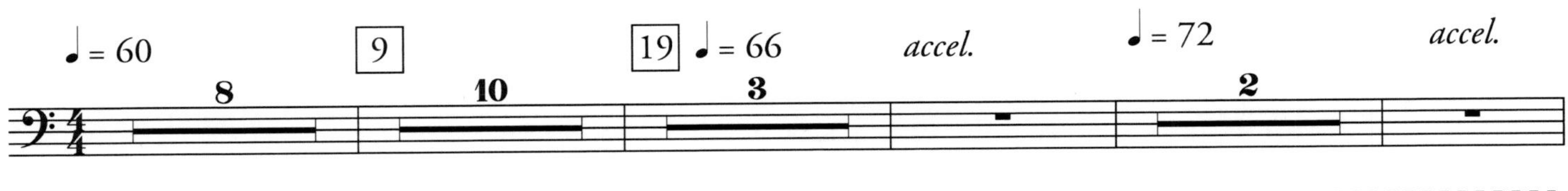

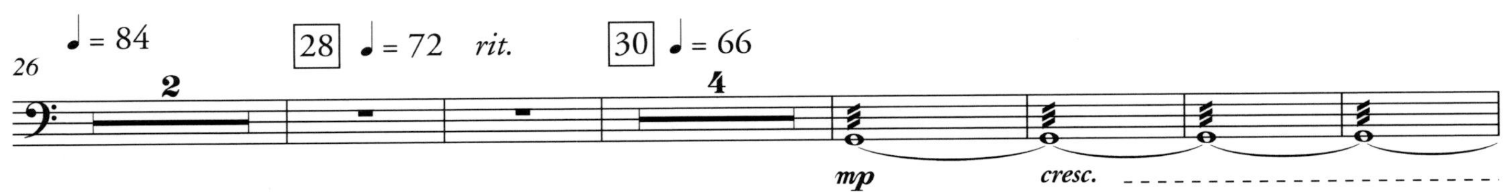

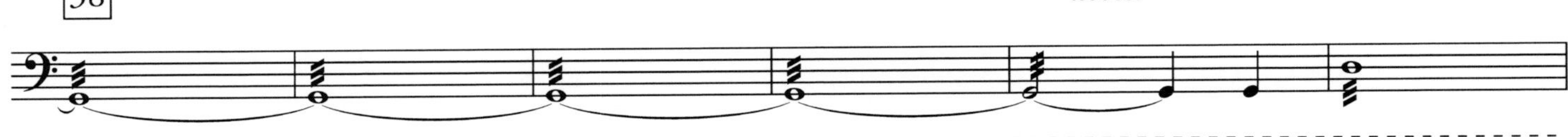

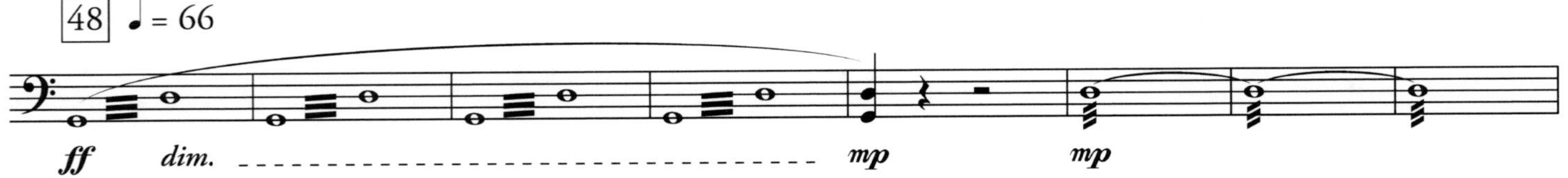

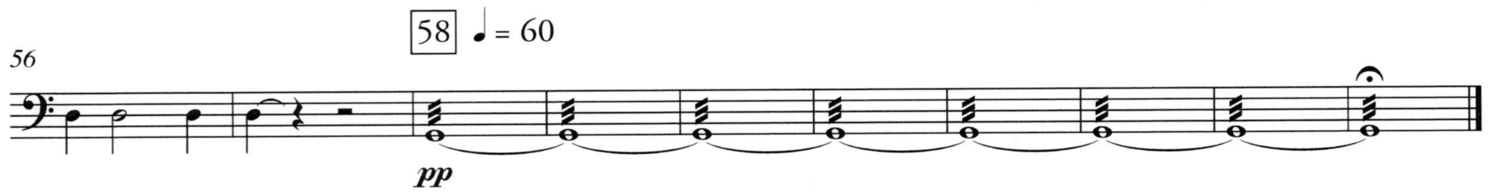

Appendix A

COMMON PERCUSSION INSTRUMENTS

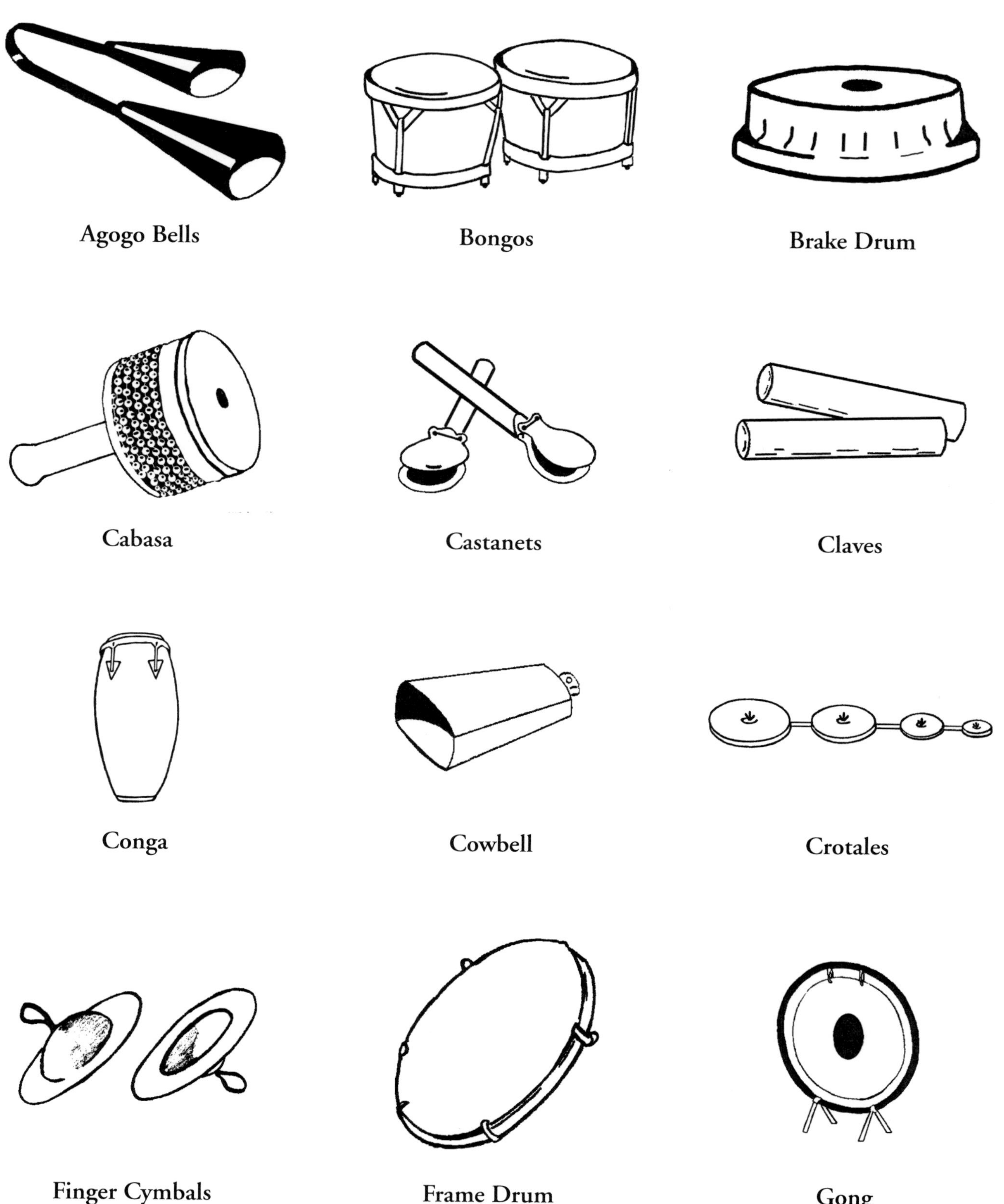

Appendix A (cont.)

Appendix B

PERCUSSION INSTRUMENT SUBSTITUTIONS

Bell Tree	Glissando on orchestra bells with hard beater
Bongos	Two high-pitched tom-toms or two snare drums tuned high
Cabasa	Maracas played with both in one hand
Castanets	Woodblock
Chimes	Orchestra bells with hard mallets in octaves or vibraphone with hard mallets
Chocalo	Maracas
Conga	Tenor drum tuned to a low pitch and played with hands
Cowbell	Bell of cymbal, muffled with the hand
Crotales	Orchestra bells
Finger Cymbals	Triangle
Hi-Hat	Crash cymbals choked together
Marimba	Xylophone player 8vb with yarn mallets
Ratchet	Rudimental roll on shell of bass drum
Slapstick	Rim shot on snare drum or ruler struck flat on table top
Tambourine	Snare drum or sleigh bells
Tam-Tam	Large suspended cymbal
Temple Blocks	Set of varied sounding woodblocks
Tenor Drum	Low concert tom
Timbales	Two snare drums without snares
Timpani	Bass drum if only one pitch
Tom-Tom	Snare drum without snares
Triangle	Dome of cymbal
Vibraphone	Orchestra bells played 8vb
Woodblock	Shell of bass drum or snare drum
Xylophone	Marimba played 8va using hard mallets